The Shrimp Lover's Cookbook

by

William G. Flagg

N NORTH RIVER PRESS, INC.

© Copyright 1984 by William G. Flagg. All rights reserved. Except for brief quotes for review purposes, no part of this work may be reproduced or transmitted in any form or by any means, electronic or mechanical, including photocopy, recording, or any information retrieval system, without written permission from the publisher.

Manufactured in the United States of America

Library of Congress Cataloging in Publication Data

Flagg, William G., 1934–
   The shrimp lover's cookbook.

   1. Cookery (Shrimp) I. Title.
TX753.F54 1984   641.6'95   84-7957
ISBN 0-88427-055-6

Credits

It must be confessed, at the outset, that this book is not entirely my creation. Credit must be given to the many friends who shared favorite shrimp recipes for inclusion. Special thanks to Agnes Inocencio, who put up with both my moods during its preparation, and with the sharing of many of the recipes tested. A good typist is also essential, especially when your spelling is as bad as mine; Toni Murray fulfilled this role . . . and added many constructive suggestions. Thanks also to the smartest woman in the world . . . my mom . . . who can spot a misspelled word from a mile away, for her efforts in proofreading. Lastly, my appreciation is given to Cory Wild, the artist who created the shrimp characters that grace these pages. Without the contributions of this group, this book you are holding could never have been created.

Other North River Press Titles by William G. Flagg

- The Clam Lover's Cookbook
- The Mushroom Lover's Cookbook

PREFACE

My teens were spent in a small town called North Attleboro, in Massachusetts. My dad ran "Flagg's Bakery". About the time I started Junior High School he handed me a broom, taught me how to clean the floor, got me a wooden box to stand on, taught me how to grease the muffin tins and wash all the pots and pans, gave me a raise in my allowance, and somehow taught me about "pay" and that my "allowance" was a thing of the past.

At about this time, a portly Italian gentleman (who never forgot a name), named Ori Scarlatelli, opened a fine restaurant called "The Brook Manor". It was a truly luxurious restaurant, housed in a converted mansion. My dad and Ori became friends and did business with each other. Dad would supply the rolls and special cakes to the restaurant and the Flagg family would get to eat at this elegant restaurant about twice a month.

What has all this to do with a shrimp cookbook? Well, The Brook Manor served the best shrimp cocktail in the world, and that's where I first learned to love shrimp. It was served in a cocktail glass, on a bed of crisp, shredded lettuce, with a cocktail sauce rich with horseradish that was so fresh it would sometimes make your eyes water. And the shrimp, jumbo of course, were cold and as crispy as could be. I'd eat all the shrimp, and then gobble down all the lettuce, still covered with that hot, spicy cocktail sauce. Oh, my, it was good!

I went back there this past summer. My dad's dead now and Ori has long since retired, but his son is at the door (and he, too, never forgets a name). Would you believe the shrimp cocktail is just the same as I remembered it! (Who said you can't go back!)

The shrimp cocktail is what started me on the road which eventually led me to write the book you are now holding.

It has been much more than a pleasure to do the research necessary to compile this book. Some of the recipes have been favorites of mine for many years, others have been developed by me recently, and many have been shared by my friends (for sure, I'm not the only shrimp lover). But from whatever source, what I have tried to assemble is a collection of the best shrimp recipes in the world, written in a clear, easy to follow style, so that, regardless of one's skill in the kitchen, my fellow shrimp lovers can all prepare delicious shrimp delicacies to their hearts' content. Enjoy!!

                              William G. Flagg

Guide to Contents

- Introduction VI
- Basics of Cooking Shrimp 1
- Appetizers ... Served Hot 11
- Appetizers ... Served Cold 17
- Pickled and Marinated 25
- The First Course 31
- Bisques, Gumbo, Jambalaya 39
- Salads 47
- Sandwiches 55
- Cooked on the Grill 63
- Deep Fat Fried Favorites 69
- Shrimply Delicious Main Dishes 87
- Sauces to Dip your Shrimp 105
- Detailed Contents 113

INTRODUCTION

In the last fifty years, shrimp have become the most universally popular seafood item in the United States. More pounds of shrimp are sold than lobster or any other one kind of fish or shellfish. Their taste, the fact that they freeze well, may be transported and distributed rapidly, and seem to be available in limitless quantities are the secrets of the shrimp's meteoric rise to fame. As to which is the most popular shrimp dish, that depends upon what authority you read. It seems, however, that the contest "boils" down to either Shrimp Cocktail or Deep-Fried Breaded Shrimp.

WHAT SHRIMP ARE

Shrimp and prawns are small, slender crustaceans with ten jointed legs attached to the thorax and swimmerets attached to abdominal segments. The body is compressed laterally and the thin, smooth, almost transparent exoskeletons are shed periodically as the shrimp or prawn matures.

The term prawn is applied loosely to large shrimp but, although they resemble shrimp, they are not of the same family. A true prawn has a strong body and tail, a toothed beak (rostrums) with a prominent grooved head, long antennae and slender legs.

Shrimp and prawns can grow to a length of nine inches but are usually found much smaller.

Scampi is the Italian name for a class of orange-colored, shrimplike shellfish found in the Adriatic.

Tiny brine shrimp that are smaller than one inch belong to a completely different sub-class of crustaceans and are not true shrimp.

Shrimp swim rather than crawl, unlike their relatives, the lobsters and crabs. They are also able to swim backward quickly with their paddle-like tails.

In American waters the shrimp are grayish-green or greenish-brown. A few species found on the Gulf Coast are pink. Most brown shrimp found in markets are from Brazil.

All shrimp and prawns turn pink and white when cooked and there is little or no difference in flavor or texture. Both shrimp and prawns have lean flesh with a firm white texture. Both are an excellent source of minerals . . . calcium, phosphorous, sulfur and copper . . . high in iodine and protein and low in calories. They have a few water soluble vitamins.

WHAT TYPES ARE AVAILABLE?

The types of shrimp caught along the shores of the United States primarily consist of the blue, brown, California Bay, northern, rock and white. Crawfish include the freshwater crawfish, sea crawfish, and western crayfish.

WHERE ARE THEY CAUGHT IN THE U.S.?

Shrimp and prawns are abundant in temperate and tropical, fresh, and salt waters. In the United States, large commercial catches are made off the coasts of Virginia, Louisiana, and in the Gulf of Mexico.

WHEN CAN THEY BE PURCHASED?

Shrimp are available all year round. The peak of the season for average size is August through December; for jumbo sizes, March through June.

IN WHAT FORMS ARE THEY SOLD?

Fresh raw in shells: Some shrimp and prawns are shipped to market between layers of ice. The majority are frozen by the packer and then shipped to your market. Your dealer then thaws them before he sells them. They are neither shelled nor deveined, but normally the head is removed.

Fresh cooked shrimp: You can find fresh cooked shrimp in some stores, sold by the pound. Normally, shrimp purchased in this fashion will be shelled and deveined. Before buying, ascertain that they are refrigerated or packed in ice.

Packaged frozen shrimp: These may be raw (a) in the shell, (b) in shells, deveined or (c) shelled and deveined. They also may be purchased cooked (a) in the shells or (b) shelled and deveined.

Frozen shrimp are available in a variety of package sizes, among them 8 ounces, 12 ounces, 16 ounces and larger. These shrimp are individually frozen and come shelled, either "ready to cook" or "ready to serve". Shrimp size is not specified on the package nor is the number per pound. Instead; "all purpose", "cooked salad", or "salad and cocktail" is the description the consumer if offered. The size of the shrimp, however, can be viewed through the package.

Packaged Frozen, breaded shrimp: These are shelled and deveined, either uncooked or cooked and ready to reheat. Frozen stuffed jumbo shrimp are also available.

Canned: These are cooked in their own juices and packed, either dry or in brine, in 4 1/2 to 5 ounce cans (drained weight). The shrimp which are canned are either "tiny" or "medium". Always drain them and allow them to refresh in cold water for 15 minutes.

WHAT SIZES ARE SOLD?

Shrimp are sold by the number of shrimp (headless, with shells on) to the pound. The heads are normally removed shortly after shrimp are caught. The following describes a typical procedure for classifying shrimp: A shrimp boat comes in to the dock of a packer. The shrimp are unloaded via conveyor belt. As they pass by an inspector, he periodically picks off several shrimp and weighs them. The average number per pound become the "count" for that batch.

GRADING OF SHRIMP.

Apparently, there is no U.S. standard for grading shrimp. Each market . . . New York, Chicago, and Gulf ports, for example, each have their own classifications. The following Table is a composite of these and others, but should provide a good guide.

NUMBER PER POUND	SIZE OR GRADE NAME
U-9 (under 9/pound)	Giant or Colossal
U-12 (under 12/pound)	Giant or Colossal
U-16 (under 16/pound)	Extra Jumbo
16-20	Jumbo
21-25	Large
26-30	Large/Medium
31-35	Medium
36-40	Medium/Small
41-45	Medium/Small
46-50	Medium/Small
51-55	Small
56-60	Small
61-70	Small
71-80	Very Small, Titi
80-200	Very Small, Titi
200 or more	Minature, Danish or Cocktail

WHAT SIZE SHOULD I PURCHASE?

Since all sizes of shrimp may be used interchangeably in most recipes, except those that call for the larger sizes, the size of the shrimp assumes more importance if the cost and time required to prepare a recipe are taken into consideration. For example, jumbo or large shrimp generally cost the most but take less time to peel and devein. This size is appropriate for stuffed shrimp, butterflying, broiling, and deep-fat frying. Small shrimp cost less but take longer to prepare. Use small shrimp in salads, casseroles and creamed dishes. Regardless of size, all shrimp have the same fine flavor and food value.

HOW MUCH SHOULD I BUY?

The answer to this question will vary somewhat depending upon appetizers and the richness of the dish. However, a good guide is 3/4 pounds of shrimp in shells for 2 servings. Therefore, 2 1/4 pounds of raw, headless shrimp in shells should be purchased to provide a main dish for six persons, when combined with other foods. The yield will be about 50% and 2 1/4 pounds of raw, headless shrimp in shells will yield just about three cups of cleaned, cooked shrimp.

As an example, for one cup (about 6 ounces) of cleaned, cooked shrimp (2 main course servings), purchase the following:

- 3/4 pound raw shrimp in shells, or
- 1 package (7 ounces) frozen, peeled shrimp, or
- 1 can of shrimp (7 ounces including water) will equal 4 1/2 ounces drained.

For a first course dish, 8 ounces of raw shrimp in shells will feed two. When planning appetizers, allow up to 2 ounces of raw shrimp in shells per person.

HOW DO I CHECK FOR FRESHNESS?

Raw shrimp should be firm and have a tight fitting shell around the body. Any shrinkage of the flesh can be a sign of staleness. The shells of fresh shrimp will range in color from gray to light pink. They should be moist and sweet smelling and if there is the slightest smell of ammonia, the shrimp are not fresh.

HOW LONG WILL THEY LAST?

Raw shrimp are very perishable and should be used within a day or two after being purchased from a reliable market. Cook and refrigerate them if you need to store them for a longer time. Once they have been cooked, they will keep for three to five days in a refrigerator.

Shrimp are one of the few seafood products that can be frozen without damage to their flavor or quality. They will keep in a freezer for 6 to 12 months. Keep packaged frozen shrimp in original container and store at 0°F.

To freeze shrimp: Remove heads and wash fresh shrimp thoroughly. (1) Pack shrimp closely together. Freeze in small packages wrapped in moisture-vapor-proof wrapping material. Wrap tightly, excluding as much air as possible and properly label as to date and contents. (2) Place shrimp in a moisture proof, tight sealing bag. Fill the bag with water to cover the shrimp and then freeze. Empty milk cartons may also be used. Shrimp (or any seafood) frozen in this manner does not dry or get freezer burns.

Previously frozen and thawed shrimp should not be refrozen. This causes a loss in flavor and texture changes. Previously frozen shrimp that have thawed may be refrozen after cooking. They will keep up to 3 months in the freezer.

WHEN TO REMOVE THE SHELL

Raw shrimp (fresh or quick frozen) may be shelled either before or after cooking. There are advocates of both procedures.

PRO ARGUMENTS

The sand vein is easier to remove when shrimp are raw.

The odor of cooking shrimp will not be as strong if they are shelled before cooking.

The shrimp will appear plumper if shelled first.

CON ARGUMENTS

Not so, they say; it's easier to shell and devein after cooking.

The shrimp will have more "natural" flavor if cooked in the shell.

Actually . . . it really makes little difference, so you may take your choice. If you elect to shell them before cooking, here are the directions.

TO REMOVE THE SHELL.

First, wash the shrimp. Let frozen shrimp stand in cold water for about 15 minutes, until they separate. To shell shrimp, first remove the tiny legs. Next, hold the tail end of the shrimp in your left hand. Starting at the large end, peel away the thin shell, unwinding it from around the tail. Then, still holding firmly to tail, pull the shrimp out from the remaining section and tail.

As an option, the tail section may be left intact to enhance the appearance or to use as a handle when serving shrimp as appetizers.

TO DEVEIN SHRIMP

The black vein in shrimp is harmless, but removing it, either before or after cooking, makes the shrimp more attractive.

To remove the sand vein (a process called deveining), take a knife and make a shallow incision (about 1/8 inch deep), along the outside curvature. With the knife point (or a toothpick) lift out the black sand vein in one piece.

Then, rinse away any broken bits of vein under cool running water. Pat dry with paper towels, or drain and place in refrigerator to chill until ready to use.

TO BUTTERFLY SHRIMP

This step is most often done when shrimp are to be stuffed or dipped in batter and deep fat fried. Butterflying is done before shrimp are cooked.

Deepen incision made for deveining, cutting almost but not quite through the underside.

Spread shrimp as flat as possible (like an open book) and pat dry with paper towels.

Some recipes call for broiling butterfly shrimp in the shell. To do this, devein and slit the shrimp while in the shell, or slice the shrimp in half lengthwise, leaving the shrimp intact at the tail end.

WHAT ARE THE QUALITIES OF WELL COOKED SHRIMP?

- Coral or pink colored exterior, white interior.
- A well-cleaned body.
- A perfectly retained shape, firm to the touch.
- A delicate aroma, sweet smelling.
- A "spring" or resilience to the tail.
- A succulent appearance, neither too moist nor too dry.

SALT, PEPPER AND BUTTER

In the recipes that follow, measurements have been given for salt and pepper. You should, however, use salt and pepper to taste whenever possible. Also, as I am an incurable "butter monster", all recipes call for butter. If you prefer to substitute margarine . . . that's up to you.

Basics of Cooking Shrimp

The tail of the shrimp is the only part eaten. The head and thorax are usually removed before the shrimp reach the market. Occasionally, along the southeastern or gulf coasts, they can be purchased with the head still attached. In this case, the head is normally removed before cooking.

If the water the shrimp are to be cooked in is to be used for stock (or if the shrimp are cooked in a sauce) be certain to wash the shrimp off before cooking.

All the recipes in this book direct the cook to cook shrimp for the shortest possible time, just until they turn pink. This is undoubtedly the most important instruction in this book. Cooking shrimp longer (10-15 minutes) toughens them and cooking them for a really long time (say 1 hour) turns them into a tasteless mush.

In my research for this book, I found that recipes which were written 30 or 40 years ago (for dishes such as gumbo) called for boiling shrimp in the sauce for up to an hour or more. The same recipe written today would call for the raw shrimp to be added about 5 minutes before serving the dish.

By cooking the shrimp for the minimum possible time, they will be cooked to perfection, yet retain their own identity, in terms of flavor or chewiness.

I've found some recipes call for putting shrimp in cold water, heat the water to a boil, then time the cooking for 3 to 4 minutes. This method will also result in perfectly cooked shrimp, but to me, there is some danger that the cook might be occupied with some other task at the moment that the water begins to boil and, therefore, not have a good fix on the exact moment to begin the timing.

By putting the raw shrimp into boiling water, even people who have a limited attention span (like me) can keep an eye on the pot while the water comes back to a boil.

Obviously, the larger the quantity of water in relation to the quantity of shrimp and the hotter the heat source under the pot, the faster the water will return to a boil.

Three topics are presented in this section . . . . .

- Basic ways of cooking shrimp, for use in cocktails, salads and other dishes which call for cooked shrimp. (Other methods such as sauteeing, frying in deep-fat, or grilling are discussed in other sections of this book.)

    - Cooking Shrimp Before Removing Shells . . . 3
    - Cooking Shrimp After Removing Shells 4

- A variety of recipes for cooking shrimp in some great spicy mixes. You'll love 'em.

    - Hot and Spicy Steamed Shrimp 5
    - Shrimp Boil 7
    - Garithes (Shrimp) in Shells 8

- Periodically, it's nice to have a shrimp flavored broth. You'll find appropriate recipes here.

    - Shrimp Cooked in Court Bouillon 9
    - Shrimp Shell Broth 10

Cooking Shrimp Before Removing Shells

INGREDIENTS (for each pound of shrimp)

1	Pound	Raw shrimp, fresh or frozen, in shells
4	Cups	Water
2	Tbsps.	Salt

DIRECTIONS

- If frozen, leave shrimp in their package and allow to thaw overnight in the refrigerator, or thaw them under a gentle stream of cold running water.

- Once shrimp are thawed, wash them off and allow them to drain well.

- Combine water and salt in a pot and bring to a rolling boil.

- Add the shrimp and stir once, to ascertain that any shrimp still slightly frozen are separated. Allow water to return to a boil, cover the pot, reduce heat, and allow the shrimp to simmer for 2 to 3 minutes (if small) up to 4 or 5 minutes (if jumbo), just until the shells turn pink.

- Remove from heat and pour the shrimp into a colander. Discard the cooking liquid. Run cold water over them to quickly cool.

- Shell and devein the shrimp. Rinse them under cool running water and pat dry with paper towels. Refrigerate them until time to use.

Cooking Shrimp After Removing Shells

INGREDIENTS (for each pound of shrimp)

1	Pound	Raw shrimp, fresh or frozen, in shells
4	Cups	Water
1	Tbsp.	Salt

DIRECTIONS

- If frozen, leave shrimp in their package and allow to thaw overnight in the refrigerator, or thaw them under a gentle stream of cold running water.

- Shell and devein the shrimp. Rinse well and allow to drain.

- Combine water and salt in a pot and bring to a rolling boil.

- Add the shrimp and allow the water to return to a boil. Cover the pot, reduce the heat, and allow the shrimp to simmer for 2 to 3 minutes (if small), up to 4 to 5 minutes if jumbo, <u>just</u> until outside of shrimp turn pink.

- Remove from heat and pour the shrimp into a colander Discard the cooking water. Run cold water over them to quickly cool. Pat them dry with paper towels. Refrigerate them until time to use.

Have you ever been at a cocktail party, at a seafood bar, or enjoying a few beers at a backyard picnic, when some kind soul brought out a large bowl of unshelled steamed shrimp?

Did you notice how suddenly the crowd gathers around that bowl and everyone gets busy with both hands cleaning shrimp as fast as possible, popping them into their mouths as soon as they are cleaned, washing them down with frosty beer or an icy-spicy Bloody Mary . . . . yet the conversation seems, if possible, more animated than before the shrimp arrived!

Yes, this has to be one of the most popular ways of enjoying shrimp. And to help you join in the fun, here's a recipe for preparing this treat.

Hot and Spicy Steamed Shrimp

INGREDIENTS (serves 6)

2 1/4	Pounds	Raw shrimp, fresh or frozen, in shells
3	Tbsps.	Seafood Seasoning
1	Tbsp.	Shrimp Spice
1	Tbsp.	Kosher salt (large crystals)
1	Tsp.	Cayenne pepper
1/2	Cup	Vinegar
1/2	Cup	Water

DIRECTIONS

- If frozen, soak the shrimp until thawed and separated. Wash and drain well.

- Combine the Seafood Seasoning, Shrimp Spice, salt and Cayenne pepper. Mix well.

- Place a layer of shrimp in a steamer basket. Sprinkle generously with the spicy mixture. Continue layering in the shrimp and the spice mixture, ending with the spices.

- Place the vinegar and water in the bottom of the steamer and heat to a rolling boil.

HOT AND SPICY STEAMED SHRIMP (continued)

- Place steamer basket over boiling vinegar water and cover. Allow to steam for 3 to 5 minutes, just until shrimp turn pink.

- Quickly remove basket and pour the shrimp, together with its spice blend, into a serving dish. Do not rinse with cold water.

- Serve immediately with napkins and lots of cold beer. Let each guest shell their own shrimp.

NOTES

- Seafood Seasoning: Available in supermarkets . . . contains salt, celery seed, red pepper, spices, mustard flour and paprika.

- Shrimp Spice: Available in supermarkets . . . contains mustard seed, dill seed, ginger, red pepper, bay leaves, cloves, allspice, cassia and black pepper.

Shrimp Boil

INGREDIENTS (serves 6)

2 1/4	Pounds	Raw shrimp
1	Tbsp.	Shrimp Spice (or more)
2	Quarts	Water
4	Tsps.	Salt

DIRECTIONS

- Shell and devein the shrimp. Rinse under cold running water and allow to drain.

- Tie the shrimp spice in a cheesecloth and drop into water. Bring water to a boil and allow to simmer for 15 minutes.

- Add the salt and the shrimp. Cover and return to a boil. Allow to simmer for 3 to 4 minutes, just until shrimp turn pink.

- Remove pan from heat and pour shrimp into a colander. Remove spices in cheesecloth. Allow to drain but do not rinse.

- Serve either hot or cold with your favorite sauce.

NOTES

- Shrimp Spice: Available in supermarkets . . . contains mustard seed, dill seed, ginger, red pepper, bay leaves, cloves, allspice, cassia and black pepper.

- As a variation, substitute Pickling Spice in place of Shrimp Spice. Pickling Spice is also available in supermarkets . . . contains cinnamon, allspice, mustard seed, coriander, bay leaves, ginger, chilies, cloves, black pepper, mace and cardamon.

If you find yourself in the Greek Islands, here's a recipe they use to prepare shrimp there. Listen... can't you almost hear the music?

Garithes (Shrimp) in Shells

INGREDIENTS (serves 6)

2 1/4	Pounds	Raw shrimp in their shells
2	Cloves	Garlic, mashed
6	Sprigs	Parsley
1	Cup	Dry white wine
1/2	Cup	Olive oil
1	Tsp.	Salt
1/4	Tsp.	Black pepper, freshly ground

DIRECTIONS

- Rinse the shrimp briefly under running cold water and set them aside to drain.

- Combine remaining ingredients in a large saucepan. Bring to a boil over moderate heat and boil for 1 minute.

- Remove the saucepan from the heat, add the shrimp and stir for 1 minute, to baste them with the wine and herbs.

- Return the saucepan to the heat, bring the liquid to a boil and simmer the shrimp uncovered for 3 minutes, just until they turn pink, stirring occasionally.

- Remove the saucepan from heat and allow the shrimp to cool in the juices.

- Chill the shrimp and then drain before serving.

To give shrimp a bit of extra flavor and to obtain shrimp-flavored broth, additional ingredients are added during cooking, as in this recipe.

Shrimp Cooked in Court Bouillon

INGREDIENTS (for 1 pound shrimp)

1	Quart	Water
1/2	Rib	Celery, chopped
1	Medium	Carrot, sliced
1	Small	Onion, sliced
1/8	Cup	Lemon juice (1/2 lemon)
1	Tsp.	Salt
1/4	Tsp.	Black pepper, freshly ground
1	Pound	Raw shrimp, fresh or frozen, with or without shells

DIRECTIONS

- Put the water in a saucepan. Add all remaining ingredients except shrimp. Bring the water to a boil.

- Add shrimp and let the water come to a boil again. If shrimp were frozen, stir with a fork to ascertain they have all separated. Turn heat down so water just simmers. Cover saucepan and simmer for 2 minutes (if shrimp are small) to 3 minutes (if shrimp are large), just until shrimp turn pink.

- Drain shrimp and cool quickly. Reserve liquid for use as flavor in soups, sauces, etc.

Don't throw away those shrimp shells. They can become your secret ingredient in 100 other dishes.

Shrimp Shell Broth

INGREDIENTS (makes about 1 1/2 quarts broth)

1/2	Pound	Shrimp shells, from 2 pounds of shrimp, uncooked
2	Quarts	Water
1	Rib	Celery, chopped
1	Medium	Onion, chopped
1	Medium	Carrot, chopped
1	Tsp.	Salt

DIRECTIONS

- After peeling shrimp, place some of the shells in a mortar. Crush them thoroughly with a pestle. Add some of the water and mix well. Pour the shell-water mixture into a 4 quart saucepan. Repeat this process until all shells and 2 quarts of water have been used.

- Add the celery, onion, carrot and salt to the shell-water mixture. Cover, bring to a boil and simmer for 30 to 45 minutes.

- Line a large sieve with two thicknesses of cheese-cloth, which has been wet and wrung out. Place the seive over a mixing bowl.

- Strain the shell-water mixture through the cheese-cloth. Lift up the edges of the cheese-cloth, capturing the shells in the center. Gather the edges of the cheese-cloth together and wring out the last bit of liquid. Transfer broth to a refrigerator storage container and allow to cool.

- Cover and refrigerate, or freeze, until ready to use, as added flavoring for sauces, soups and stir fry dishes. It should keep for 1 week in the refrigerator or for 3 months in freezer.

Appetizers
. . . Served Hot

- Shrimp and Cheese Canapes 12
- Shrimp Stuffed with Crab Meat 13
- Shrimp Rumaki 14
- Shrimp Toast 15

Shrimp and Cheese Canapes

INGREDIENTS (makes 20 appetizers)

1/2	Cup	Shrimp, cooked, peeled, deveined and chopped (about 1/4 pound frozen shrimp in shells)
1	Cup	Swiss cheese, shredded
1/2	Cup	Fresh bread crumbs (1 slice)
1/3	Cup	Mayonnaise
1	Tsp.	Lemon juice
1/4	Tsp.	Salt
1/8	Tsp.	Thyme
20	Slices	Party rye bread (or crisp crackers)
		Fresh dill (for garnish)

DIRECTIONS

- In a small mixing bowl, combine the shrimp, cheese, bread crumbs, mayonnaise, lemon juice, salt and thyme.

- Spoon small amounts of the shrimp mixture onto the bread slices. Place canapes on rack of broiler pan.

- Broil, about 6" from heat source, for 9 or 10 minutes, until mixture is hot and tops are lightly browned.

- Garnish with bits of dill and serve immediately.

HINT

- Make up the shrimp mixture in advance. Cover and refrigerate until ready to assemble and broil.

Shrimp Stuffed with Crab Meat

INGREDIENTS (makes 32)

1/2	Cup	Butter
1	Tbsp.	Onion, minced
1	Tbsp.	Green pepper, minced
4	Drops	Tabasco sauce
1/2	Tsp.	Worcestershire sauce
1	Tsp.	Salt
1/8	Tsp.	Black pepper, freshly ground
1	Cup	Flour
2	Cups	Half-and-half
2	Packages	Frozen crab meat (6 ounces each), thawed, drained and flaked
32	Jumbo	Shrimp, fresh or frozen (about 2 pounds)

DIRECTIONS

- Heat butter in a large saucepan over medium heat. Add onion and green pepper. Saute until tender. Stir in the Tabasco and Worcestershire sauces and the salt and pepper.

- Stir in the flour until blended. Gradually add the half-and-half, stirring continually, until a smooth sauce has formed. Simmer sauce gently for 10 minutes, stirring periodically.

- Stir in the crab meat, cover, and set aside to cool.

- Peel and devein the shrimp. Split shrimp butterfly style. Arrange them in a buttered baking dish, cut side up.

- Spoon the sauce over the shrimp.

- Bake, in a preheated 350° oven, for 20 to 25 minutes, until shrimp are cooked and sauce is lightly browned.

- Serve with melted butter and lemon wedges.

Shrimp Rumaki

INGREDIENTS (makes 24)

24		Raw jumbo shrimp, shelled and deveined (1 1/2 pounds)
1	Cup	Soy sauce
1	Cup	Medium-sweet sherry
1	Tsp.	Fresh ginger root, finely grated
12	Slices	Bacon, halved crosswise

DIRECTIONS

- Place the shrimp in a bowl. Add the soy sauce, sherry and ginger. Mix well and marinate, in refrigerator, for 2 to 3 hours, turning periodically.

- Drain marinade from shrimp and reserve.

- Cook the bacon until half done (not crisp). Drain. Wrap a piece of bacon around each shrimp and secure with a toothpick. Arrange shrimp on a rack in a large shallow baking pan.

- Broil for about 4 minutes, basting 1 or 2 times with the reserved marinade.

- Turn the shrimp and continue broiling, basting 1 or 2 times, for an additional 4 minutes, until bacon is nicely browned and shrimp are cooked.

- Transfer to a serving dish and serve immediately.

Shrimp Toast

INGREDIENTS (makes 60)

1	Pound	Raw shrimp, shelled and deveined
1	Can	Water chestnuts (5 ounce), drained
1/4	Cup	Green onion (green part only), chopped
2	Tsp.	Salt
1	Tsp.	Sugar
1		Egg, beaten
15	Slices	White bread (thin)
1/2	Cup	Dry bread crumbs
		Oil for frying

DIRECTIONS

- With the finest blade of your grinder, or with a blender, grind together the shrimp, water chestnuts and green onions. Add the salt, sugar and egg. Blend thoroughly.

- Spread this mixture on the slices of bread. Sprinkle lightly with bread crumbs and cut each slice into four triangles.

- Pour oil into a frying pan to a depth of 1 inch. Heat oil until very hot. Fry each triangle, shrimp side down first, then brown the other side. Drain on paper towels.

HINT

- These delicious appetizers may either be served immediately or frozen for a future meal. When ready to serve, defrost and reheat at 400°F for five minutes.

Appetizers
... Served Cold

- Shrimp and Vegetable Appetizer 18
- Stuffed Shrimp Canape 19
- Roquefort Stuffed Shrimp 20
- Shrimp Stuffed Eggs 21
- Shrimp Stuffed Celery 22
- Shrimp Pate 22
- Shrimp Butter 23

Shrimp and Vegetable Appetizer

INGREDIENTS (serves 12, as one of several appetizers)

2	Cups	Mayonnaise
1/2	Cup	Commercial sour cream
2	Tbsps.	Prepared horseradish, drained
2	Tbsps.	Mustard powder
1/2	Tsp.	Salt
1	Tbsp.	Lemon juice, freshly squeezed
1	Dozen	Cherry tomatoes
1	Small	Cucumber, peeled, cut into 4 wedges, and then cut crosswise into 1/2 inch triangles
1		Green bell pepper, cut into 4 wedges, stem and seeds removed, and then cut into 1 inch squares
1	Can	Whole water chestnuts (4 ounce), drained and each cut in half
1		Avocado, seed removed and peeled, and cut into 1 inch squares
1	Pound	Medium shrimp (about 36), cooked, peeled, deveined, rinsed and chilled.

DIRECTIONS

- In a large serving bowl, combine the mayonnaise, sour cream, horseradish, mustard, salt and lemon juice.

- Gently stir in the vegetables and shrimp. Chill until ready to serve.

NOTE

- Provide guests with bamboo skewers for spearing.

Stuffed Shrimp Canape

INGREDIENTS (makes 24)

12	Medium	Shrimp, cooked, peeled and deveined, split in half down the middle of the back
1/2	Cup	French dressing
12	Slices	Sandwich bread
4	Tbsps.	Butter, softened
1	Tbsp.	Chives, chopped
4	Tbsps.	Mayonnaise
4	Tbsps.	Parsley flakes
6		Anchovy filets, cut into fourths
8	Tbsps.	Caviar
1/4	Cup	Lemon juice (1 lemon)

DIRECTIONS

- Prepare the shrimp as indicated. Place them in a glass bowl and add the French dressing. Toss lightly and allow the shrimp to marinate in refrigerator for two hours.

- Cut two rounds (1 1/2" to 2") from each slice of bread.

- Cream the butter and chives together. Spread this mixture on bread rounds. Spread a layer of mayonnaise over the butter and then edge the bread rounds with parsley.

- Drain the shrimp and place one rounded half shrimp on each bread round. Insert a piece of anchovy filet into each shrimp and top with a teaspoon of caviar. Squeeze a few drops of lemon juice on each canape and serve.

Roquefort Stuffed Shrimp

INGREDIENTS (makes about 24)

2	Quarts	Water
1	Tsp.	Salt
2	Pounds	Large fresh (or frozen) shrimp
1	Package	Cream cheese (3 ounces)
1	Ounce	Roquefort (or blue) cheese
1/2	Tsp.	Prepared mustard
1	Cup	Fresh parsley, finely chopped

DIRECTIONS

- In a 4 quart saucepan, heat the water and salt to a boil. Add shrimp and cover. Return the water to a boil, then lower heat and simmer gently until shrimp just turn pink, 3 to 4 minutes.

- Drain and peel the shrimp, leaving the tails attached (optional) to use as handles. Split each shrimp part way down along back (curved surface). With a knife point, remove the vein in one piece. Rinse shrimp quickly in cold running water. Pat dry with paper towels. Chill.

- Blend together the cream cheese, Roquefort cheese and mustard. Chill.

- Using a pastry tube (or small spoon), stuff the shrimp (inside the curve) with the cheese mixture. Roll the cheese side in parsley. Arrange on platter and serve.

For perfect hard-cooked eggs, follow this recipe.

Shrimp Stuffed Eggs

INGREDIENTS (makes 12)

6		Eggs
1/4	Cup	Mayonnaise
2	Tbsp.	Cooked shrimp, finely chopped
2	Tbsp.	Celery, finely chopped
1/4	Tsp.	Salt
1/8	Tsp.	Black papper, freshly ground

DIRECTIONS

- Place eggs in a large pan, so they are not crowded. Fill the saucepan with cold water to cover eggs by at least one inch.

- Over high heat, heat until water is fully boiling. Remove pan from heat, cover tightly and allow to stand for 15 minutes. Pour off water and place pan under running cold water. (This prevents the eggs from forming an unattractive grayish-green ring around the yolk, caused by overcooking.)

- Crack shells all around and peel eggs. Slice eggs in half lengthwise. Gently remove yolks and place in a small bowl.

- With a fork, gently mash yolks. Add mayonnaise, shrimp, celery, salt and pepper. Stir until thoroughly mixed.

- Spoon mixture into egg centers. Cover loosely and refrigerate until time to serve.

- Garnish with a thin slice of stuffed olive and serve.

HINT

- For the best hard-cooked eggs, buy eggs several days before you cook them, or use your oldest eggs. Very fresh eggs are difficult to peel after cooking.

Shrimp Stuffed Celery

INGREDIENTS (makes about 24)

1	Can	Shrimp (7 ounce), drained and chopped
1/3	Cup	Mayonnaise
1 1/2	Tsps.	Lemon juice
2	Tsps.	Parsley flakes
1 1/2	Tsps.	Onion, finely diced
1/4	Cup	Crushed pineapple
1	Tbsp.	Walnuts, chopped
1/4	Tsp.	Salt
4	Drops	Tabasco sauce
6	Stalks	Celery (about 8" long)
		Paprika

DIRECTIONS

- Combine the shrimp, mayonnaise, lemon juice, parsley, onion, pineapple, walnuts, salt and Tabasco sauce. Mix well.

- Stuff the celery stalks with this mixture. Sprinkle with paprika. Cut into 2" lengths. Arrange on a platter and serve.

Shrimp Pate

INGREDIENTS (makes 2 cups)

3/4	Pound	Small shrimp, cooked, peeled and well drained, finely diced
1	Small	Onion, finely diced
1	Package	Cream cheese (3 ounces), cut into cubes
1/3	Cup	Mayonnaise
1	Tbsp.	Horseradish
1	Tbsp.	Lemon juice
1	Tsp.	Dijon-style mustard
1/4	Tsp.	Tabasco sauce
1	Tsp.	Dry dill
1/2	Tsp.	Sugar
1/2	Tsp.	Salt
		Crackers or bread rounds

DIRECTIONS

- Combine all ingredients and mix until well blended. Shape into a ball or spoon into a crock.

- Refrigerate for a few hours or overnight, to allow flavors to blend. May be refrigerated for two days, but do not freeze.

- Serve pate with crackers or bread rounds.

Shrimp Butter

INGREDIENTS (makes about 2 cups)

1/2	Pound	Butter (2 sticks), softened
3/4	Pound	Shrimp, cooked, peeled, deveined, and minced
1/4	Tsp.	Salt
1/8	Tsp.	Paprika
1	Tbsp.	Lemon juice

DIRECTIONS:

- Combine all ingredients in a small mixing bowl and mix thoroughly. If the mixture is not entirely smooth, rub through a sieve.

- Spread on toast rounds and garnish appropriately, or use as a base for sandwich fillings.

Pickled
and Marinated

The following dishes may be served as either an appetizer or as a first course. When purchasing shrimp for use as an appetizer, plan on up to 2 ounces of raw shrimp in shells for each person . . . and, as a first course, about 4 ounces of raw shrimp in shells for each serving.

- Pickled Shrimp 26
- Marinated Shrimp 27
- Italian Style Marinated Shrimp 28
- Deviled Shrimp 29
- Cold Spiced Szechwan Shrimp 30

Pickled Shrimp

INGREDIENTS

2	Pounds	Frozen raw shrimp in the shell
1/2	Cup	Celery leaves, chopped
1/4	Cup	Whole mixed pickling spice
2	Quarts	Water, boiling
2	Cups	Onions, sliced
1 1/2	Cups	Vegetable (or olive) oil
1 1/2	Cups	White vinegar
5		Bay leaves
2	Tbsps.	Capers, with liquid
1 1/2	Tsps.	Celery seed
1 1/2	Tsps.	Salt
1/4	Tsp.	Tabasco sauce

DIRECTIONS

- Thaw, peel and devein the shrimp. Wash in cold water.

- Cook the celery leaves and pickling spice together for 10 minutes in the boiling water. Add the shrimp and simmer, covered, for 3 to 4 minutes, just until shrimp turn pink. Drain.

- In a glass or pottery bowl, arrange layers of shrimp and onion. Combine the oil, vinegar, bay leaves, capers, celery seed, salt and Tabasco sauce. Pour this mixture over the shrimp and onions.

- Cover and refrigerate overnight. Drain before serving.

HINT

- Serves 8 as a first course on shredded lettuce, or, as an appetizer in a bowl with toothpicks, it will serve up to 16.

Prepare this dish the day before your next party.

Marinated Shrimp

INGREDIENTS (serves up to 16, as an appetizer)

2	Pounds	Raw shrimp, shelled and deveined
3/4	Cup	Olive oil
1/2	Cup	Onion, chopped
2	Cloves	Garlic, minced
2	Tsp.	Salt
1/4	Tsp.	Black pepper, freshly ground
1	Tsp.	Paprika
1/2	Cup	Cider vinegar
1/4	Tsp.	Dry mustard
1/8	Tsp.	Ground red pepper (cayenne)
1	Large	Onion, thinly sliced

DIRECTIONS

- Wash shrimp and pat dry with paper towels.

- Heat 1/4 cup oil in skillet. Add onion and garlic. Saute for about 5 minutes. Add shrimp, 1 teaspoon of salt, the pepper and paprika. Saute for 5 minutes and cool for 20 minutes.

- Mix together the remaining oil and salt, the vinegar, mustard and the red pepper.

- Arrange layers of shrimp and sliced onion in a bowl and pour marinade over it all. Cover and allow to marinate in refrigerator for 24 hours.

- When serving, remove shrimp from marinade and put on toothpicks.

Italian Style Marinated Shrimp

INGREDIENTS (serves up to 24, as an appetizer)

3	Pounds	Shrimp, cooked, shelled and deveined
1/2	Cup	Olive oil
1/2	Cup	Wine vinegar
1	Jar	Pimentoes (3 ounces)
2		Hot cherry peppers, finely chopped
2	Cloves	Garlic, minced
1	Tsp.	Salt
1/2	Tsp.	Black pepper, freshly ground
1/4	Tsp.	M.S.G. (optional)
1/2	Cup	Grated Romano cheese
1	Package	Cream cheese (8 ounces)
1/2	Bottle	Capers

DIRECTIONS

- Place shrimp in a bowl. Combine all remaining ingredients, mix well and pour over shrimp. Toss to thoroughly coat shrimp.

- Cover and refrigerate. Allow to marinate overnight or longer. Stir often to mix. Drain before serving.

- Provide toothpicks for spearing.

Deviled Shrimp

INGREDIENTS (serves 8 as a first course)

2	Pounds	Raw shrimp in the shell
1		Lemon, thinly sliced
1		Red onion, thinly sliced
1/2	Cup	Pitted ripe olives
2	Tbsps.	Pimento, chopped
1/2	Cup	Lemon juice, freshly squeezed
1/4	Cup	Salad oil
1	Tbsp.	Wine vinegar
1	Clove	Garlic, minced
1		Bay leaf, broken
1	Tbsp.	Dry mustard
1/4	Tsp.	Cayenne pepper
1/2	Tsp.	Black pepper, freshly ground
1	Tsp.	Salt

DIRECTIONS

- Shell and devein the shrimp. In a large saucepan, bring water to a boil. Add the shrimp, let water return to a boil, reduce heat, cover and simmer the shrimp for 3 to 4 minutes, just until they turn pink. Drain at once.

- In a mixing bowl, combine the shrimp, lemon slices, onion, olives and pimento.

- In another bowl, combine the remaining ingredients. Stir into the shrimp mixture. Cover and refrigerate overnight. To serve, spoon from bowl onto small plates, or provide toothpicks for spearing.

Cold Spiced Szechwan Shrimp

INGREDIENTS (serves 3 to 6)

1/2	Pound	Medium raw shrimp (about 16)
1	Tbsp.	Fresh ginger, minced
4	Whole	Green onions, finely chopped
1	Tbsp.	Dry sherry
1	Tsp.	Salt
1	Tsp.	Szechwan (or whole black) peppercorns
1 1/4	Cups	Water (approximately)

DIRECTIONS

- Wash unshelled shrimp and place them in a small saucepan. Add ginger, onion, sherry, salt and peppercorns. Barely cover with water.

- Bring water to a boil, then cover pan and reduce heat. Simmer the shrimp for 3 to 4 minutes, just until they turn pink.

- Chill the shrimp in the stock, then shell and devein. Return to stock, cover and chill. Drain stock before serving.

HINT

- Serve as part of an appetizer cold plate.

The First Course

- Shrimp Cocktail 32
    - Seafood Cocktail Sauce 33
- Shrimp Remoulade 34
- Mushroom and Shrimp Cocktail 35
- Garlic Shrimp 36
- Baked Garlicky Breaded Shrimp 37
- King Stuffed Shrimp 38

... And when I get to heaven, I'm going to have shrimp cocktail three times a week ... no, make that four times a week ... and here's the recipe:

Shrimp Cocktail

INGREDIENTS (serves 4)

1	Quart	Water
2	Tbsps.	Salt
1	Pound	Raw shrimp in shells (about 32 medium or 24 large)
4	Crisp	Lettuce leaves
1	Cup	Lettuce, shredded
1	Cup	Shrimp Cocktail Sauce (next page)
4	Wedges	Lemon

DIRECTIONS

- Combine the water and salt in a two quart saucepan. Bring the water to a boil. Add the shrimp, cover and return to a boil. Reduce heat and cook for 2 to 3 minutes, until shrimp just turn pink. Drain, shell and devein the shrimp. Rinse with cold water and pat dry with paper towels. Chill.

- Line the bottom and sides of a stemmed cocktail glass with a piece of lettuce. Add some shredded lettuce to make a "bed" for the shrimp.

- Place 1 or 2 shrimp on the shredded lettuce and arrange the remainder around the edge of the glass, with tails hanging over the edge.

- Spoon about 1/4 cup of sauce over the shrimp which are in the center of each glass.

- Place the cocktail glass on a flat dish. Add a wedge of lemon, which has been pierced with a seafood fork and serve.

I dare not tell you how much horseradish (and it must be fresh) that I use in this recipe, but I have been known to bring a tear or two to the eye of an unsuspecting guest. Actually, except for one or two habits like this, I'm really quite dependable.

Seafood Cocktail Sauce

INGREDIENTS (makes about 1 scant cup)

3/4	Cup	Catsup (or chili sauce)
2	Tbsps.	Prepared horseradish, drained
1	Tbsp.	Lemon juice
1/2	Tsp.	Salt (or celery salt)
1/8	Tsp.	Black pepper, freshly ground
1/2	Tsp.	Worcestershire sauce
1/8	Tsp.	Tabasco sauce (or cayenne pepper)

DIRECTIONS

- Combine all ingredients. Pour into plastic container. Cover and refrigerate until well chilled.

I first had shrimp prepared this famous French way in New Orleans. Being a New Englander, I still favor a tangy cocktail sauce, but this has to be a close second.

Shrimp Remoulade

INGREDIENTS (serves 6)

1 1/2	Pounds	Raw shrimp, peeled and deveined, with tail shell left intact
1	Cup	Mayonnaise
1	Clove	Garlic, finely chopped
1	Small	Onion, finely chopped
1		Egg, hard-cooked and finely chopped
1		Dill pickle, finely chopped
4	Tbsps.	Parsley flakes
1	Tsp.	Dry mustard
1	Tsp.	Tarragon
1/2	Tsp	Paprika
1	Tsp.	Black pepper, freshly ground
		Boston lettuce

DIRECTIONS

- Drop the shrimp into boiling, salted water. Return the water to a boil and allow to simmer for 4 minutes. Drain immediately and chill shrimp thoroughly.

- In a mixing bowl, combine the mayonnaise, garlic, onion, hard-cooked egg, dill pickle, parsley flakes, dry mustard, tarragon, paprika and pepper. Mix thoroughly and refrigerate for at least one hour.

- For each serving, fill the bottom half of stemmed glasses with crisp Boston lettuce and arrange several shrimp around the edge, with tails hanging out. Scoop some of the sauce onto the lettuce in each glass and serve with cocktail forks. The shrimp are speared with the forks, and then dipped into the sauce.

Mushroom and Shrimp Cocktail

INGREDIENTS (serves 4)

1	Quart	Water
2	Tbsps.	Salt
1/2	Pound	Small raw shrimp (about 30) in shells
1/2	Pound	Small whole fresh mushrooms
1/2	Cup	Olive oil
3	Tbsps.	Wine vinegar
1/4	Tsp.	Dry mustard
1/8	Tsp.	Sugar
1/8	Tsp.	Salt
1/8	Tsp.	Black pepper, freshly ground
2	Tsps.	Parsley flakes
8		Crisp lettuce leaves

DIRECTIONS

- In a two quart saucepan, combine the water and salt. Bring to a boil, add the shrimp, cover and return to a boil. Reduce the heat and cook shrimp for 2 to 3 minutes, until they just begin to turn pink. Drain, peel, devein, quarter, rinse and pat the shrimp dry with paper towels. Refrigerate.

- Wipe the mushrooms clean with a damp cloth. Trim stems and slice the mushrooms thinly. Refrigerate.

- In a small bowl, combine the olive oil, vinegar and mustard. Beat until the mixture emulsifies. Add the sugar, salt and pepper. Refrigerate.

- Just before serving add the shrimp, mushroom slices and parsley to the dressing. Toss until shrimp and mushrooms are thoroughly coated.

- Arrange the lettuce leaves on 4 salad dishes. With a slotted spoon, divide the shrimp-mushroom mixture among the dishes. Serve immediately.

Garlic Shrimp

INGREDIENTS (serves 2)

1/2	Cup	Olive oil
2	Cloves	Garlic, peeled and sliced
1		Dried red chili pepper, broken into 3 pieces, seeds removed
1		Bay leaf
4	Ounces	Medium/small fresh shrimp (about 10), shelled

DIRECTIONS

- Heat the olive oil over a medium high flame in a small frying pan. Add the garlic, chili pepper and bay leaf. Heat until garlic begins to sizzle and turn golden.

- Add the shrimp and cook, while stirring, for about 2 minutes, until shrimp are cooked.

- Serve immediately, with crusty bread for dunking. Remove bay leaf before serving.

Baked Garlicky Breaded Shrimp

INGREDIENTS (serves 2)

10	Jumbo	Raw shrimp (about 1/2 pound)
6	Tbsps.	Butter
3	Cloves	Garlic, finely diced
1/2	Cup	Dry bread crumbs
1	Tbsp.	Parsley flakes
1/4	Tsp.	Salt
1/8	Tsp.	Black pepper, freshly ground
1/8	Tsp.	Cayenne pepper
2	Tsps.	Lemon juice

DIRECTIONS

- Peel the shrimp leaving the tip of the tail section intact and devein them. Rinse them under cold running water and pat dry with paper towels. With a sharp knife, split the shrimp lengthwise down the back, without cutting through. Press shrimp out flat into the shape of a butterfly. Arrange the shrimp in the bottom of a well buttered one quart baking dish, with tips of tail section sticking up around edge of dish.

- Melt the butter over medium heat in a small saucepan. When hot, add the garlic. Cook for a few seconds and then remove the pan from heat.

- Stir in the bread crumbs, parsley flakes, salt, black and cayenne peppers.

- Spoon this mixture over the shrimp. Sprinkle with the lemon juice.

- Bake, in a preheated 375° oven, for 10 minutes, until bread crumb topping is hot and golden brown.

- With a spatula, transfer 5 shrimp with their topping to each serving dish. Serve immediately.

King Stuffed Shrimp

INGREDIENTS (serves 2 as a main dish, or 4 as a first course)

1	Pound	Large raw shrimp (about 24)
1/4	Pound	King crab meat
1/4	Pound	Butter, softened (but not melted)
3	Cups	Dry bread crumbs
1/2	Cup	Dry sherry
1/8	Tsp.	Garlic powder
1/4	Tsp.	Salt
1/8	Tsp.	Black pepper, freshly ground

DIRECTIONS

- Peel and devein the shrimp. Rinse them off and pat dry with paper towels. Cut them open in a butterfly split. Lay the shrimp on their backs in an oiled baking dish.

- In a mixing bowl, combine the crab meat, butter, bread crumbs, sherry, garlic powder, salt and pepper. Stuff the shrimp with this mixture.

- Bake, in a preheated 375° oven, for 10 minutes. Serve with a cup of drawn butter.

Bisques, Gumbo, Jambalaya

- Shrimp Bisque 40
- Shrimp Bisque, Traditional 41
- Shrimp Gumbo 42
- Shrimp Jambalaya 44

Easy to make . . . and so good. It's one of my favorites.

Shrimp Bisque

INGREDIENTS (serves 6)

3	Tbsps.	Butter
1	Small Rib	Celery, finely diced
1	Small	Onion, finely diced
3	Tbsps.	Flour
4	Cups	Milk
1	Pound	Shrimp, cooked, shelled and deveined, finely mashed (about 1 1/3 cups)
1/2	Tsp.	Salt
1/8	Tsp.	White pepper
Few Grains		Nutmeg
		Paprika

DIRECTIONS

- Melt butter in a medium saucepan, add celery and onion, and cook over low heat for 5 minutes. Stir in the flour.

- Add the milk, a little at a time, while stirring constantly, until a smooth sauce has formed. Simmer gently for 10 minutes.

- Add the shrimp, salt, pepper and nutmeg. Reheat and serve, garnished with a sprinkle of paprika.

VARIATION

- Serve cold.

This more traditional bisque recipe calls for quite a few more ingredients, but it's really not at all difficult.

Shrimp Bisque

INGREDIENTS (makes about 2 1/2 quarts)

2	Cans	Tomatoes (16 ounces each)
2	Cups	Beef stock (or bouillon)
1	Cup	Celery with leaves, diced
2	Small	Onions, diced
2	Small	Carrots, diced
2	Sprigs	Parsley
4		Whole cloves
6		Whole black peppercorns
1	Small	Bay leaf
1/8	Tsp.	Thyme
2	Tsps.	Salt
3	Tbsps.	Uncooked rice
1 1/2	Pounds	Shrimp, cooked, shelled, deveined and cut into pieces
1	Pint	Light cream
		Sherry
		Croutons
		Chopped parsley

DIRECTIONS

- In a large kettle, combine the tomatoes, beef stock, celery, onions, carrots, parsley, cloves, peppercorns, bay leaf, thyme, salt and rice. Bring to a boil and simmer for one hour.

- Remove bay leaf. Force mixture through a sieve, or blend smooth with an electric blender.

- Just before serving, add shrimp and reheat.

- Heat cream (do not allow to boil) and add to bisque. Check seasonings. Add salt and freshly ground black pepper as desired.

- Serve at once, with sherry and croutons. Garnish with chopped parsley.

There are many versions of Gumbo (derived from an African word for okra, a key ingredient). Somewhere between a soup and a stew, the traditional southern method calls for a "roux" made from shortening (or oil) and flour. Also required is the seasoning Gumbo File (ground sassafras leaves). It should be hotly seasoned and served with bowls of hot, cooked rice... which is spooned into each serving.

Shrimp Gumbo

INGREDIENTS (serves 8)

1/2	Cup	Shortening (or cooking oil)
1 1/2	Pounds	Small okra pods, washed, trimmed, and sliced 1/2" thick, or 2 (10 ounce) packages frozen sliced okra (unthawed)
3	Tbsps.	Flour
1	Cup	Onion, diced
3	Cloves	Garlic, minced
1	Cup	Boiling water
2	Can	Tomatoes (1 pound, 12 ounces), with liquid
2		Bay leaves
2	Tsps.	Salt
1/2	Tsp.	Black pepper, freshly ground
1/2	Tsp.	Tabasco sauce (or more)
1	Tsp.	Worcestershire sauce
2	Pounds	Raw shrimp, shelled and deveined
1/4	Tsp.	Gumbo File powder*

DIRECTIONS

- Melt shortening over medium heat in a large Dutch oven. Add okra and saute for about 5 minutes, stirring frequently, until golden brown. Drain okra on paper towels and reserve.

- Add flour and cook, stirring frequently, until mixture turns light brown, the color of a paper supermarket bag. (This brown paste is called a "roux".)

* Available at Gourmet stores.

- Add the onion and garlic. Saute until onion is limp, about 3 minutes.

- Stir in the boiling water. Then add the tomatoes, bay leaves, salt, pepper, Tabasco sauce and Worcestershire sauce.

- Simmer, uncovered, for 20-25 minutes, stirring occasionally, until thickened and flavors are well blended.

- Add reserved okra and the shrimp and simmer for 3 minutes, just until shrimp turn pink.

- Remove from heat, take out the bay leaves, stir in the file powder and serve. Do not allow to boil after adding file.

VARIATIONS

- Add 2 pounds fresh crabmeat (which has been picked over and any cartilage discarded) when the raw shrimp are added.

- Add one pint of shucked oysters (with liquid) when shrimp are added. Simmer just until oysters curl at the edges, about 3 minutes.

After gumbo, the most famous Creole-Cajun stew is Jambalaya. The word is believed to be derived from "jambon" which means ham in both Spanish and French, and "alaya", an African expletive which can be interpreted as either acclaim or derision.

Jambalaya started out as a poor man's catch-all... utilizing any leftover meats, sausage, shrimp or fish that might be available and stretching them a long way with plenty of rice.

Shrimp Jambalaya

INGREDIENTS (serves 6 to 8)

2	Pounds	Raw shrimp, fresh or frozen
1	Pound	Small link sausages, cut into 1/2" lengths
1 1/2	Cups	Smoked ham, diced into 1/2" cubes
1/4	Cup	Butter (1/2 stick)
1		Green bell pepper, stem and seeds removed, chopped
2	Medium	Onions, chopped (about 1 cup)
2	Cloves	Garlic, minced
2	Cups	Uncooked rice
1	Cup	Beef or chicken broth
1	Can	Tomatoes (1 pound 13 ounces)
1/2	Tsp.	Salt
1/4	Tsp.	Black pepper, freshly ground
1/4	Tsp.	Cayenne pepper (or more)
1		Bay leaf

DIRECTIONS

- Cook the shrimp in Court Bouillon. (Recipe is elsewhere in this book.) Shell and devein the shrimp. Cut shrimp in half.

- Cook sausage over medium heat in a large skillet, stirring frequently, until browned. With a slotted spoon, remove sausage and reserve. Pour off all but 2 tablespoons of fat. Add smoked ham and cook, stirring frequently, until browned. With a slotted spoon, remove the ham and reserve.

- Add butter to remaining fat in pan. Add the pepper, onion and garlic. Cook over low heat until onion is tender and slightly browned.

- Add the rice and cook, stirring frequently, until rice is browned.

- Stir in the broth and tomatoes. Break up the tomatoes somewhat. Add the salt, pepper, cayenne and bay leaf. Bring to a boil, reduce heat, cover skillet and cook very slowly for about 30 minutes, until rice is cooked. If mixture becomes too dry, add a bit of water.

- When rice is cooked stir in the shrimp, sausage, and ham, reserving some for garnish. Taste and adjust seasonings if desired.

- Pour mixture into a greased casserole, removing bay leaf in the process. Top with the reserved shrimp, sausage and ham. Bake, in a preheated 425° oven, for 10 minutes.

VARIATIONS

- Use bacon (3 slices), diced, instead of sausage links.

- Add pieces of chicken, shucked oysters, crab meat, or what have you. (A jambalaya is almost never made the same way twice and just about any way is good.)

- After adding the tomatoes and spices, this dish may be finished in the oven. Stir in most of the shrimp, sausage and ham. Sprinkle the remainder on top, cover and bake, in a preheated 350° oven, until rice is tender, about 1 and 15 minutes.

Salads

- Shrimp Salad 48
- Stuffed Tomato Salad 49
- Shrimp in Avocado Halves 50
- Party Shrimp Salad 51
- Shrimp and Macaroni Salad 52
- Shrimp and Pineapple Salad 53
- Shrimp Mousse 54

Shrimp Salad

INGREDIENTS (serves 4)

1	Pound	Shrimp, cooked, shelled, deveined and diced
2	Stalks	Celery, diced
1	Medium	Onion, finely diced
2		Hard cooked eggs, diced
1/2	Tsp.	Salt
1/4	Tsp.	Black pepper, freshly ground
2	Tbsps.	Lemon juice
1/3	Cup	Mayonnaise
4		Fresh tomatoes
		Lettuce

DIRECTIONS

- Toss together the shrimp, celery, onion, eggs, salt, pepper, lemon juice and mayonnaise.

- Quarter tomatoes and place each on a bed of crisp lettuce leaves. Arrange salad on tomatoes.

Ever eat uncooked asparagus? Delicious! It must be really fresh. Use only the upper half of stalk, rinse thoroughly . . . and try this dish.

Stuffed Tomato Salad

INGREDIENTS (serves 6)

6	Large	Ripe tomatoes
1 1/2	Pounds	Shrimp, cooked, shelled and deveined
1	Cup	Raw asparagus, cut up
2	Tbsps.	Celery, diced
1	Tsp.	Chopped chives
1/2	Cup	Mayonnaise

DIRECTIONS

METHOD #1:

- Cut a thin slice from the top of each tomato. Using a small spoon, scoop out the seeds and pulp, leaving shells about 1/4 inch thick. (Use tomato centers in sauce or salad at another time.) Sprinkle insides with salt and pepper. Invert shells on paper towels to drain.

METHOD #2:

- Cut whole tomato into petals by making 3 cuts with a sharp knife. Do not cut all the way through tomato. First cut in half, then make 2 additional cuts in each half to form 6 petals. With a spoon, scoop out seeds and pulp. Sprinkle insides with salt and pepper. Carefully turn upside down on paper towels to drain while preparing filling.

- Combine remaining ingredients. Fill tomatoes with this filling. Garnish top of salad with a swirl of mayonnaise and a slice of stuffed olive.

Shrimp in Avocado Halves

INGREDIENTS (serves 6)

1	Pound	Cooked shrimp, small or medium size (2 pounds raw, or use 4 (4 1/4 ounces, drained weight) cans tiny or medium shrimp, drained
1/2	Cup	French dressing (recipe elsewhere in this book)
3	Medium	Ripe avocados, chilled
1/2		Lemon
		Water cress

DIRECTIONS

- Peel and devein shrimp. Place them into a bowl and pour the French dressing over them. Toss lightly to evenly coat the shrimp with the dressing.

- Cover and place in refrigerator to chill and marinate. Toss shrimp occasionally.

- Just before serving time, rinse the avocados, cut them in half lengthwise and remove the seeds.

- Squeeze the juice from the lemon onto the cut surfaces of the avocados.

- Pile the shrimp into the avocado halves, dividing them equally. Garnish each with sprigs of water cress and serve.

Party Shrimp Salad

INGREDIENTS (serves 12)

4	Pounds	Shrimp, shelled and deveined, cooked and chilled
2	Packages	Frozen peas (6 ounces each), cooked as package directs, drained and cooled
1	Small	Onion, finely diced
1	Cup	Celery, diced
2		Green bell peppers, stem and seeds removed, diced
1 1/2	Cups	Mayonnaise
3/4	Cup	Sweet pickle relish, well drained
1/4	Cup	Parsley, minced
1 1/2	Tsp.	Salt
1/2	Tsp.	Black pepper, freshly ground
2	Heads	Boston lettuce, washed and chilled
12	Sprigs	Parsley
9		Eggs, hard cooked, sliced

DIRECTIONS

- In a large bowl, combine the shrimp, peas, onion, celery, peppers, mayonnaise, relish, parsley, salt and pepper. Toss lightly until well mixed.

- Line a large salad bowl with the crisp lettuce leaves. Arrange salad in bowl and garnish with parsley and egg slices.

Shrimp and Macaroni Salad

INGREDIENTS (serves 10)

2	Cups	Cooked macaroni
1/2	Tsp.	Salt
1/4	Tsp.	Black pepper, freshly ground
1/2	Cup	Mayonnaise
2	Tbsps.	Sweet pickle, finely chopped
5		Ripe olives, finely chopped
5		Hard cooked eggs, chopped
1/2	Cup	Onion, finely chopped
1/2	Cup	Celery, finely chopped
2	Pounds	Shrimp, cooked, shelled and deveined, cut into bite-sized pieces

DIRECTIONS

- Combine all ingredients except shrimp. Mix well, place in a covered dish and chill.

- About 30 minutes before serving, stir in shrimp and toss lightly.

Shrimp and Pineapple Salad

INGREDIENTS (serves 6)

1	Can	Pineapple chunks (16 ounces) drained
1 1/2	Pounds	Shrimp, cooked, shelled and deveined, cut into quarters
1	Cup	Mayonnaise
		Lettuce
		Paprika

DIRECTIONS

- In a small bowl, combine the pineapple, shrimp and half the mayonnaise.

- Serve on lettuce leaves, topped with mayonnaise and a sprinkle of paprika.

VARIATION

- Apple and/or orange, diced, are also good in combination with shrimp.

Shrimp Mousse

INGREDIENTS (serves 4)

1	Package	Gelatin
1/4	Cup	Cold water
1	Can	Condensed tomato soup (10 3/4 ounces)
1	Package	Cream cheese (8 ounces)
1/2	Cup	Mayonnaise
2	Stalks	Celery, chopped
1/2	Cup	Onion, grated
1/4	Cup	Green bell pepper, finely chopped
1/2	Pound	Bite-size shrimp, cooked and cleaned
1/4	Tsp.	Salt
1/8	Tsp.	Black pepper, freshly ground
1/8	Tsp.	Seasoned salt
4	Drops	Hot pepper sauce

DIRECTIONS

- Dissolve gelatin in the cold water. Heat the tomato soup and add to the gelatin. Cool this mixture, stirring periodically.

- When cool, add the cream cheese and beat with an electric beater at low speed.

- Add remaining ingredients and stir to thoroughly mix. Pour into a cold, wet 2 quart mold and refrigerate for 3 to 4 hours before serving.

- Unmold and garnish with salad greens.

Sandwiches

- Shrimp Salad Sandwiches 56
- Shrimp-Avocado Club Sandwiches.......... 57
- Ham and Baby Shrimp Sandwiches 58
- Broiled Shrimp Sandwiches 59
- Shrimp, Bacon and Cheese Sandwiches....... 60
- Shrimpburgers 61

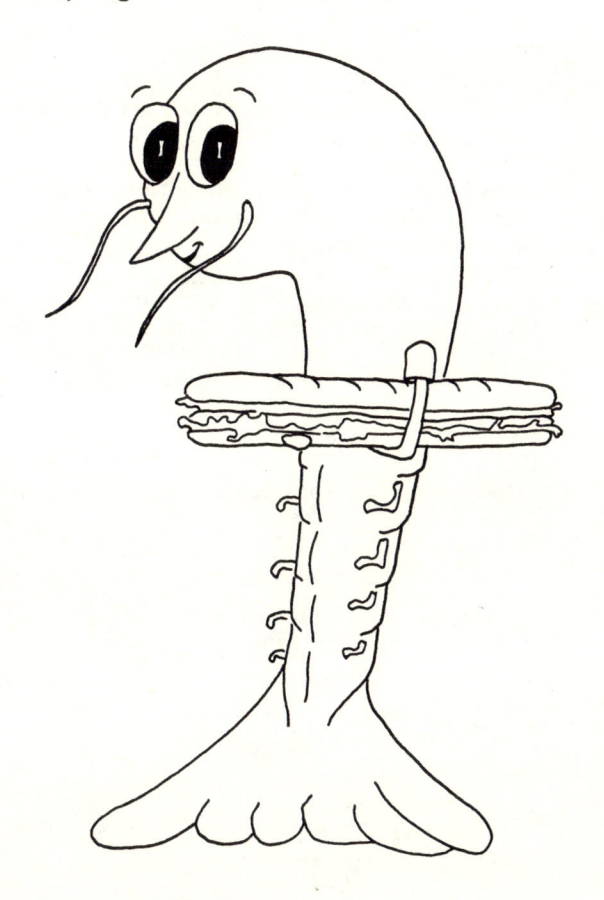

Shrimp Salad Sandwiches

INGREDIENTS (makes 4 to 6)

3/4	Pound	Shrimp, cooked, shelled, deveined and cut into 1/2" pieces
1	Tsp.	Lemon juice
1/4	Cup	Onion, finely diced
1/2	Cup	Celery, finely diced
1/4	Tsp.	Salt
1/8	Tsp.	Black pepper, freshly ground
		Mayonnaise
		Fresh bread, sliced
		Butter
		Lettuce

DIRECTIONS

- Combine and toss together the shrimp, lemon juice, onion, celery, salt and pepper. Chill.

- Just before assembling sandwiches, drain shrimp mixture and then add just enough mayonnaise to moisten.

- Spread bread slices with soft butter. Generously cover half the bread slices with the filling. Top each with a slice of crisp lettuce and the remaining bread slices.

VARIATIONS

- Use hamburger, hot dog, or bulky rolls rather than bread.

Shrimp-Avocado Club Sandwich

INGREDIENTS (makes 1)

3	Slices	Buttered toast
1/4	Pound	Shrimp, cooked, shelled and deveined (sliced on the diagonal, if large)
		Salt
		Black pepper, freshly ground
2	Tsp.	Mayonnaise
1/4		Avocado, peeled, seeded and sliced
2	Slices	Crisp bacon, cut in half

DIRECTIONS

- Cover bottom layer of toast with shrimp. Sprinkle lightly with salt and pepper.

- Cover with the second piece of toast, buttered side down.

- Spread with mayonnaise. Arrange sliced avocado and bacon.

- Top with the third slice of toast. Pat gently in place.

- Stick a toothpick into each of the four sides through the three pieces of toast. Cut the sandwich diagonally both ways, making four triangular pieces.

Here's a Danish "open faced" sandwich you'll enjoy. It's eaten with knife and fork ... and you should plan more than one for each person.

Ham and Baby Shrimp Sandwich

INGREDIENTS (makes 4)

4	Slices	White bread
2	Tbsps.	Soft butter
4	Slices	Ham
4		Lettuce leaves
1	Can	Cooked baby shrimp (4 1/2 or 5 ounces, drained)
2	Tbsps.	Pickle, minced
2	Tbsps.	Mayonnaise

DIRECTIONS

- Spread the bread generously with butter. Cover each with a slice of ham, cut to fit.

- Add crisp lettuce leaves and pile the shrimp into the center.

- Trim with pickle and put a dollop of mayonnaise on top of the shrimp.

Broiled Shrimp Sandwiches

INGREDIENTS (makes 8)

4		Eggs, hard-cooked
1	Tsp.	Salt
1/8	Tsp.	Black pepper, freshly ground
1/4	Tsp	Dry mustard
1	Tsp.	Chopped chives
2	Tbsps.	Butter, melted
1		Egg yolk (discard the white)
1/4	Cup	Heavy cream
1	Can	Shrimp (4 1/2 or 5 ounces, drained)
8	Slices	Bread, toasted on one side
		Paprika
		Parmesan cheese, grated

DIRECTIONS

- Separate hard-cooked yolks from whites. Chop the whites and mash the yolk. To the yolks, add salt, pepper, mustard and chives. Stir in the melted butter, the egg yolk, cream, shrimp and the chopped egg whites.

- Spread this mixture on the untoasted sides of each of the bread slices. Sprinkle with a little paprika and Parmesan cheese.

- Arrange sandwiches on a baking sheet and broil until filling is lightly browned. Serve immediately.

These are delicious served either as "sandwiches" at lunch or as hors d'oeuvres at a cocktail party.

Shrimp, Bacon & Cheese Sandwiches

INGREDIENTS (makes 8)

4	Slices	Bacon
1	Can	Shrimp (4 1/2 or 5 ounces, drained)
1	Tbsp.	Onion, finely diced
2	Tbsps.	Celery, finely diced
1	Tbsp.	Parsley flakes
2	Tbsps.	Mayonnaise
4	Slices	Bread
4	Slices	American cheese

DIRECTIONS

- Cut bacon strips in half. In a small skillet, saute until slightly crisp.

- Drain the shrimp. Soak for 15 minutes in cold water to refresh. Drain again and pat dry with paper towels. Cut into 1/4" pieces.

- In a small bowl, combine the shrimp, onion, celery, parsley and mayonnaise. Mix well.

- Toast bread slices on one side. Cut each in half and spread the untoasted side with shrimp mixture. Top each with a half slice of cheese and a piece of bacon.

- Broil, about 4" from heat for 3 to 4 minutes, until cheese is bubbly. Serve hot.

Shrimpburgers

INGREDIENTS (makes 6)

3/4	Pound	Frozen cooked, peeled and cleaned shrimp
3	Tbsps.	Butter
3	Tbsps.	Flour
3/4	Cup	Milk
1	Cup	Cooked rice
1/2	Cup	Grated sharp Cheddar cheese
1	Small	Onion, finely diced
1	Tsp.	Salt
1/4	Tsp.	Black pepper, freshly ground
1/2	Tsp.	Curry powder
		Fine dry bread crumbs
		Shortening for frying
6		Sandwich rolls, split, toasted and buttered

DIRECTIONS

- Thaw the shrimp, then rinse and drain them. Cut them into small pieces.

- Melt the butter in a small saucepan. Blend in the flour. Add the milk, a little at a time, while stirring constantly, until a smooth sauce has formed. Allow sauce to simmer gently for about 5 minutes to cook the flour.

- Add the rice, cheese, onion, salt, pepper and curry powder. Cook over low heat until cheese has melted.

- Remove from heat, stir in the shrimp and chill.

- Shape into 6 patties. Roll in bread crumbs. Fry, in a small amount of shortening in a skillet, until golden brown on both sides.

- Serve between roll halves, with chutney if desired.

Cooked on the Grill

- Barbecued Shrimp 64
- Shrimp en Brochette 65
- Chinese Skewered Shrimp 66
- Shrimp Kebabs 67

Move over, barbecued pork ribs. A tangy barbecue sauce goes just great with shrimp.

Barbecued Shrimp

INGREDIENTS (serves 4)

1/2	Cup	Salad oil
1	Medium	Onion, diced
3/4	Cup	Catsup
3/4	Cup	Water
1/3	Cup	Lemon juice
3	Tbsps.	Sugar
3	Tbsps.	Worcestershire sauce
2	Tbsps.	Prepared mustard
2	Tsp.	Salt
1/4	Tsp.	Bottled hot pepper sauce (or more)
1 1/2	Pounds	Large fresh shrimp (about 36)

DIRECTIONS

- Heat oil in a quart saucepan. Add onion and saute until tender.

- Add the catsup, water, lemon juice, sugar, Worcestershire sauce, mustard, salt and pepper sauce. Simmer uncovered for 15 minutes.

- Shell and devein the shrimp, leaving last section of shell and tail intact. Arrange shrimp on skewers.

- Brush shrimp with sauce. Rotate over hot coals until shrimp are done, 5 to 8 minutes. Brush frequently with sauce.

- Serve remaining sauce in a small bowl.

Try this scrumptious dish the next time perfect weather beckons you outside to the charcoal grill.

Shrimp en Brochette

INGREDIENTS (serves 6)

1/3	Cup	Salad oil
1/3	Cup	Lemon juice
4	Cloves	Garlic, minced
1 1/2	Tsp.	Salt
1/2	Tsp.	Paprika
1/4	Tsp.	Black pepper, freshly ground
1 1/2	Pounds	Raw shrimp (about 30), shelled and deveined
2	Medium	Green bell peppers, stems and seeds removed, cut into wedges
2	Medium	Onions, cut into wedges
12		Cherry tomatoes

DIRECTIONS

- In a mixing bowl, combine the salad oil, lemon juice, garlic, salt, paprika and pepper. Add shrimp and toss to coat. Refrigerate for at least 2 hours. Drain, reserving the marinade.

- Grease six 12" skewers. Alternate the shrimp, green pepper and onion wedges on the skewers. Brush with marinade.

- Grill, about 3 inches from heat, for about 12 minutes, turning once and brushing often with marinade.

- During last 2 minutes, place tomatoes on skewers.

Marinades combine tenderizing and flavoring agents. How well the Chinese cooks know this, as demonstrated in this mouth watering dish.

Chinese Skewered Shrimp

INGREDIENTS (serves 4)

1 1/2	Pounds	Large fresh or frozen uncooked shrimp
1/3	Cup	Dry sherry
1/3	Cup	Soy sauce
1/3	Cup	Olive oil
1	Tbsp.	Fresh ginger, finely diced
2	Cloves	Garlic, finely diced
1	Can	Water chestnuts (8 ounces), sliced
6	Slices	Bacon, cut into 6 or 8 squares

DIRECTIONS

- Shell and devein the shrimp. Wash and then pat dry with a paper towel. Place them in a mixing bowl and add the sherry, soy sauce, olive oil, ginger and garlic. Toss to blend ingredients and thoroughly coat shrimp. Allow to marinate for 30 minutes, tossing once again during this period.

- Thread the shrimp on metal skewers with sliced water chestnuts and squares of bacon.

- Grill them over hot coals for 5 to 8 minutes, turning several times and basting with the remaining marinade. Serve hot from the grill.

The brandy imparts a heavenly aroma, great flavor.

Shrimp Kebabs

INGREDIENTS (serves 6)

1 1/2	Pounds	Medium fresh or frozen shrimp
1	Pound	Fresh mushrooms
8	Slices	Bacon, cut into 6 or 8 squares
1/3	Cup	Butter, melted
2	Tbsps.	Brandy
1	Tsp.	Salt
1/4	Tsp.	Black pepper, freshly ground

DIRECTIONS

- Shell and devein the shrimp. Wash under cold water and pat dry with paper towels.

- Wipe the mushrooms with a damp paper towel, if necessary. Trim off the tip of the stem with a paring knife.

- Arrange the shrimp, mushrooms and bacon on skewers, leaving a little space around the shrimp.

- Combine the butter, brandy, salt and pepper. Brush the kebabs with this mixture.

- Cook over coals, turning a few times, until shrimp are cooked, from 5 to 8 minutes.

Deep Fat Fried Favorites

- French Fried Shrimp 70
- Deep Fried Butterfly Shrimp 71
- Shrimp in Beer Batter 72
- Fried Shrimp in Cornmeal 73
- Shrimp Tempura 74
- Szechwan Spicy Shrimp 76
- Hawaiian Shrimp Luau 78
- Crab Meat Stuffed Shrimp 79
- Shrimp Croquettes 80
- Philippine Egg Rolls 82
    - o   Egg Roll Wrappers 84

Shrimp is America's favorite seafood . . . and French fried is the Number One way of preparing them.

French Fried Shrimp

INGREDIENTS (serves 6)

2		Eggs
2	Tbsps.	Water
1/2	Cup	Fine cracker crumbs
1	Tsp.	Salt
1/8	Tsp.	Garlic powder
1/4	Cup	Flour
1 1/2	Pounds	Shrimp, shelled and deveined (about 48)
		Fat, for frying

DIRECTIONS

- Combine eggs and water. Beat until thoroughly blended.

- Combine cracker crumbs, salt, garlic powder and flour.

- Dip shrimp in eggs, then into crumb mixture. Place one layer deep in frying basket. Fry, in deep fat heated to 360°, for 3 to 5 minutes, depending upon size. Drain on paper towels.

- Serve hot with tartar, chili or cocktail sauce.

NOTES

- Previously cooked, peeled and deveined shrimp may also be French fried. Just follow the above recipe, but deep-fry for less time, about 2 to 3 minutes per batch.

- When peeling raw shrimp for use in this recipe, you may wish to leave the tail sections attached. Those tails make great handles!

Deep Fried Butterfly Shrimp

INGREDIENTS (serves 4)

1	Pound	Raw shrimp, medium or large, fresh or frozen
1/2	Cup	Milk
1		Egg
1/2	Cup	Flour
1/4	Tsp.	Baking powder
1/4	Tsp.	Salt
1/8	Tsp.	Black pepper, freshly ground
		Fat or oil (for deep frying)

DIRECTIONS

- Shell and devein the shrimp, leaving the tails on. Rinse in cold, salted water. With a sharp knife, split the shrimp lengthwise down the back, without cutting through. Press shrimp out flat in the shape of a butterfly. Pat dry with paper towels.

- Beat the milk with the egg. Combine the flour, baking powder, salt and pepper. Beat into the egg mixture.

- Heat fat in a deep fryer to hot but not smoking, 360°. Lower frying basket into the hot fat.

- Hold each shrimp by the tail and dip completely into the batter. Gently drop the shrimp, a few at a time, into the hot fat. Fry for 3 to 4 minutes, until golden brown.

- Raise basket and drain shrimp. Transfer shrimp from basket to paper towels. Keep cooked shrimp warm in a 200° oven.

- Repeat process until all shrimp are fried. Serve with lemon wedges, tartar and cocktail sauces.

No shrimp cookbook would be complete without a recipe for deep fat fried shrimp coated with a beer batter. Here's one of the best.

Shrimp in Beer Batter

INGREDIENTS (serves 2)

1	Can	Domestic light beer (12 ounces)
1 1/2	Cups	Flour
1	Tbsp.	Paprika
1/2	Tsp.	Salt
16	Medium	Raw shrimp (about 1/2 pound)
2	Tbsps.	Lemon juice
		Worcestershire sauce
		Salt
		Black pepper, freshly ground
4	Cups	Cooking oil
1	Cup	Flour

DIRECTIONS

- Pour beer into a medium bowl. Sift in the flour, paprika and salt. Stir with a wisk until batter is light and frothy. (Batter may be used at once or after standing several hours. Wisk from time to time to keep thoroughly mixed.)

- Shell the shrimp, leaving tip of tail and first segment attached, for use as a handle. Devein the shrimp, wash under cold water and pat dry with paper towels. Arrange on a platter and sprinkle with lemon juice, Worcestershire sauce, salt and a few grinds of pepper.

- Heat the oil in a fryer to 360°.

- Dredge shrimp in flour, coating completely. Grasp each shrimp by tail shell and dip into the batter, coating well.

- Drop shrimp into hot oil, one by one, and cook until golden brown and crisp. Remove with slotted spoon and allow to drain on paper towels.

Fried Shrimp in Cornmeal

INGREDIENTS (serves 4)

1	Pound	Raw medium shrimp
2		Eggs, lightly beaten
1	Cup	Cornmeal
1	Tsp.	Salt
1/4	Cup	Celery seed
		Cooking oil (for frying)

DIRECTIONS

- Shell and devein the shrimp, leaving the tail shell intact.

- Dip shrimp into beaten eggs and coat them lightly with a mixture of the cornmeal, salt and celery seed.

- Fry the shrimp, a few at a time, in cooking oil heated to 360° until they are golden.

- Drain them on paper towels and serve with Mustard Mayonnaise. (Recipe elsewhere in this book.)

Tempura, probably the best known of Japanese dishes in the West, means to fry in deep fat. The batter used should be crisp and as light as a feather. In addition to shrimp, the list of vegetables and other seafood which could be prepared in the same way is almost endless. Tempura is usually eaten in large quantities as a one-course meal. Each diner should be given tiny dishes of grated ginger and horseradish, a few lemon wedges and a sauce or two to flavor the food.

Shrimp Tempura

INGREDIENTS (serves 6)

2	Pounds	Large raw shrip in shells
		Vegetable oil (for frying)
1/2	Cup	All-purpose flour
1/2	Cup	Cornstarch
1/2	Tsp.	Salt
1		Egg
1/2	Cup	Water
		Sauces for dipping (elsewhere in book)
		o Soya Sauce
		o Hot Apricot Sauce

DIRECTIONS

- Shell and devein the shrimp, leaving the tip of the tail for use as a handle. Split the shrimp down the back, cutting almost through. Turn over and make 2 short cuts across the inner surface, to prevent them from curling up during cooking. Rinse under cold running water and pat dry with paper towels. Open to butterfly shape. Salt lightly.

- Using a deep-fat thermometer, heat oil to 360° in a deep saucepan or electric skillet.

- Sift together the flour, cornstarch and salt into a bowl.

- Beat egg with water. Pour into flour mixture and stir just until throughly combined, but do not overbeat. Batter should be a bit lumpy.

- Holding each shrimp by the tail, dip in the batter and drop gently, a few at a time, into the hot oil.

- When shrimp rise to surface, turn and cook until golden brown, about 3 minutes.

- Serve immediately, piping hot, with sauces. Allow oil to return to 360° before frying the next batch.

HINTS

- Do not make the batter in advance. Prepare it just before you are ready to cook the shrimp.

- Here's a list of just some of the vegetables which you'll enjoy served tempura style. After preparing, salt lightly before dipping into the batter.

    - Green beans, tips and strings removed, cut into 3" lengths.
    - Sweet or white potato, cut into thin slices or strips.
    - Fresh parsley clusters
    - Eggplant, peeled, cut in half lengthwise, then into 1/4" strips.
    - Zucchini, cut into thin slices or strips
    - Yellow squash, cut into thin slices
    - Carrots, cut into thin matchsticks.
    - Asparagus, cut into 3" lengths (If asparagus is fat, cut in half lengthwise.)
    - Edible pea pods
    - Green bell pepper, cut into strips
    - Broccoli or cauliflower flowerets.
    - Fresh mushrooms, quartered lengthwise

- Try these other seafoods in combination with the shrimp:

    - Crab claws, opened to expose meat
    - Scallops
    - Lobster, cut into 1 1/2" pieces
    - Squid, cut into rings
    - Fillets of white fish, cut into pieces 3" long by 1/2" wide

Szechwan, a province in Western Central China, is reknown for its hot and spicy foods. This shrimp dish is a favorite.

Szechwan Spicy Shrimp

INGREDIENTS (serves about 4 as part of a multi-dish meal)

1		Egg
2	Tbsps.	Water
6 to 8	Tbsps.	Cornstarch
1/2	Pound	Medium raw shrimp
1/8	Tsp.	Salt
3	Cups	Salad oil (for deep frying)
1/4	Tsp.	Dried chili pepper, crushed *1
2	Tbsps.	Garlic, thinly sliced
1	Tbsp.	Fresh ginger, peeled and finely diced
1	Tbsp.	Sesame oil *2
1	Tbsp.	Dry sherry (or Chablis)
2	Tbsps.	White vinegar
4	Tbsps.	Soy sauce
4	Tbsps.	Water
4	Tbsps.	Sugar
2	Tbsps.	Scallion, cut into 1/4" rounds

DIRECTIONS

- Break the egg into a mixing bowl and beat lightly. Add 2 tablespoons of water and then stir in the cornstarch. Use 6 tablespoons for a small to medium egg and up to 8 if the egg is larger. Batter should be about the consistency of thin pancake batter.

- Shell and devein the shrimp. Wash shrimp in cold running water and pat dry with paper towels. Sprinkle lightly with salt and add to batter.

- Heat oil in a wok until hot. Drop in the batter coated shrimp, one at a time. Fry about 8 at a time until the batter turns a light golden brown, about 20 seconds. Drain well and place on serving platter. Allow oil to reheat between batches.

SZECHWAN SPICY SHRIMP (continued)

- When all the shrimp have been cooked, pour off the oil in the wok, retaining only that amount which clings to the pan.

- Reheat wok and add the chili pepper, garlic and ginger. Stir fry for a few seconds and then add the sesame oil, sherry, vinegar, soy sauce, 4 tablespoons water and the sugar. Simmer for just 2 minutes and pour over the shrimp.

- Sprinkle with the scallions and serve.

HINTS

*1 Use 1/4 teaspoon dried chili pepper for a "1 alarm" sauce, 1/2 teaspoon for "2 alarm" and up to 1 teaspoon for a "3 alarm" sauce. Unless you have a fire hose handy, I'd suggest somewhere between "1 and 2 alarm".

*2 There are two types of sesame oil available in most supermarkets. The first is pure, cold pressed sesame seed and is light yellow in color. The second (and the one used in this recipe) is made from toasted sesame seeds, is dark red in color, and is used as an oriental seasoning oil.

Hawaiian Shrimp Luau

INGREDIENTS (serves 6 to 8)

2	Pounds	Raw jumbo shrimp
1/4	Cup	Lemon juice
1/4	Tsp.	Salt
1/8	Tsp.	Ground ginger
1	Tsp.	Curry powder
2	Packages	Shredded coconut (4 ounces each)
3	Cups	Flour
3	Tsp.	Baking powder
1	Tsp.	Salt
2 1/2	Cups	Milk
4	Drops	Yellow food coloring

DIRECTIONS

- Shell the shrimp, leaving the tail shell intact (for use as a "handle".) Split back of shrimp and devein.

- Mix together the lemon juice, salt, ginger and curry powder. Pour over shrimp. Marinate for 4 to 6 hours in refrigerator.

- Spread coconut thinly on a shallow baking sheet. Place in a preheated 350° oven and toast for 5 to 7 minutes, stirring often. Cool before using.

- Combine flour, baking powder, salt, milk and food coloring. Beat until smooth. The batter will be thick.

- Drain the shrimp. Coat with more flour, dip in batter and then roll in the dried coconut.

- Fry in deep fat, heated to 360°, for 3 to 4 minutes, until batter is golden and coconut is deep brown. Serve with these dipping sauces: Chinese Mustard Sauce or Soya Sauce. (Recipes elsewhere in this book.)

Crab Meat Stuffed Shrimp

INGREDIENTS (serves 20)

1/2	Cup	Cooking oil
2	Large	Onions, chopped fine
2		Green bell peppers, stem and seeds removed, chopped fine
6	Ribs	Celery, chopped fine
3	Cloves	Garlic, peeled and diced fine
1	Pound	Raw shrimp, peeled, deveined and chopped fine
1	Tsp.	Salt
1/2	Tsp.	Black pepper, freshly ground
2	Cups	Day old bread
1	Pound	White lump crab meat
1	Tbsp.	Chopped parsley
4	Pounds	Large raw shrimp, peeled and deveined (leave tail shell attached)
		Flour
1		Egg, beaten

DIRECTIONS

- Heat the oil in a large skillet. Add the onions, green peppers, celery and garlic. Saute vegetables until tender.

- Add the chopped shrimp, salt and pepper. Cook shrimp until done.

- Toast the bread and then soak in water to moisten. Squeeze out the water and then add the bread to the shrimp mixture, a little at a time, mixing well each time.

- Add the crab meat and parsley. Cook for 5 minutes, then set aside to cool.

- With a small knife, split each shrimp down the back, being careful not to cut completely through the shrimp.

CRAB MEAT STUFFED SHRIMP (continued)

- Fill back of each shrimp with the filling. Divide each shrimp into serving portions (4 or 5 shrimp per serving) and place each portion into a small plastic bag. Freeze until ready to use.

- When ready to serve, remove as many servings as required from freezer. Dip shrimp in flour, beaten egg and then flour again.

- Fry in deep fat at 360° until golden.

Shrimp Croquettes

INGREDIENTS (serves 4)

3	Tbsps.	Butter
1/3	Cup	Flour
1/2	Cup	Milk
2	Cups	Cooked shrimp, shelled and deveined, finely chopped
1	Small	Onion, finely diced
1	Tbsp.	Parsley flakes
2	Tsps.	Lemon juice
1/2	Tsp.	Salt
1/4	Tsp.	Black pepper, freshly ground
1/4	Tsp.	Paprika
1		Egg, beaten
2	Tbsps.	Water
3/4	Cup	Dry bread crumbs
		Shortening (for frying)
1	Package	Frozen peas with cream sauce (8 ounces)

DIRECTIONS

- Melt butter in a medium saucepan. Stir in the flour. Add the milk, a little at a time, over medium heat, while stirring constantly, until a smooth, very thick sauce has formed.

- Remove from heat and stir in the shrimp, onion, parsley flakes, lemon juice, salt, pepper and paprika.

- Shape the shrimp mixture into eight cones, about 1/4 cup each.

- Combine the egg and water.

- Roll the croquettes in crumbs, dip into egg mixture and roll in crumbs again.

- Heat shortening to 360°, in a deep fryer. Deep fry croquettes, a few at a time, for about 3 minutes, until brown and hot. Drain on paper towels and keep hot.

- Prepare peas as package directs. Spoon creamed peas over croquettes.

Philippine Egg Rolls

INGREDIENTS (makes 12)

1/2	Cup	Bean sprouts, cleaned and with any skins removed
2	Tbsps.	Sesame oil (or corn oil)
2	Cloves	Garlic, minced
1	Medium	Onion, finely diced
1/2	Pound	Lean pork, ground (or pork sausage, medium spicy)
1/4	Pound	Shrimp, shelled, deveined and chopped fine
1/3	Cup	Carrots, chopped fine
1/3	Cup	Celery, chopped fine
1/3	Cup	Water chestnuts (or turnips), chopped fine
1	Tbsp.	Soy sauce
1/2	Tsp.	Salt
1/4	Tsp.	Black pepper, freshly ground
1/2	Tsp.	Sugar
1/4	Cup	Raisins
1		Egg
12		Egg roll wrappers (recipe follows)
1		Egg, slightly beaten

DIRECTIONS

- Blanch bean sprouts in 2 quarts of boiling water for 1 minute. Transfer to colander and drain.

- Heat sesame oil in wok (or dutch oven).

- Add garlic and stir fry once or twice.

- Add onion and stir fry once or twice.

- Add pork, break it up into small pieces and stir fry until it has lost its pink color.

- Add shrimp and stir fry once or twice.

- Add carrots, celery, water chestnuts and stir fry for 1 minute.

PHILLIPINE EGG ROLLS (continued)

- Add soy sauce, salt, pepper, sugar and raisins. Stir fry once or twice.

- Transfer mixture to colander. Stir and allow mixture to drain and cool.

- Once cool, break egg into mixture. Toss together and allow any egg which does not stick to drain.

- Peel one wrapper from group and lay flat on work place.

- Place about 2 tablespoons of mixture about 1" from edge of wrapper.

- Fold edge of wrapper over mixture and roll once.

- Fold sides in to close ends.

- Continue rolling to end.

- Brush end with beaten egg and seal like an envelope. (May be frozen at this time.)

- Deep fry at 360° in corn oil until crisp and golden brown on both sides.

- Remove with slotted spoon and drain on absorbent towels.

Egg Roll Wrappers

INGREDIENTS (makes about 60)

3	Cups	All purpose flour
1/2	Tsp.	Salt
1	Tsp.	Oil
4 1/2	Cups	Water

DIRECTIONS

- Combine all ingredients to obtain a smooth, thin paste. Allow to stand overnight if possible.

- Heat a Teflon coated electric skillet or grill to medium hot (350°). A drop of water will "dance" when dropped on the surface of the grill.

- Dip a pastry brush into the batter. "Paint" a 6" diameter circle of batter onto the grill, in a very thin layer. Dip brush a second time and fill in center.

- In about 20 seconds, the edges of the wrapper will begin to rise off the grill. Pick it up and transfer, uncooked side up, to a dry cloth towel. Do not stack until cool or they will stick. When cool, transfer to a large plate, placing each one so that it overlaps the others. May be used immediately, or stored in refrigerator for a day or two.

Shrimply Delicious Main Dishes

- Shrimp Creole 86
- Shrimp Newburg 87
- Shrimp Rarebit 88
- Shrimp Paella 89
- Shrimp Curry 90
- Shrimp de Jonghe 91
- Shrimp-Crab Meat Fondue in Garlicky Bread Cups 92
  - Garlicky Bread Cups 93
- Stir Fried Shrimp and Pea Pods 94
- Shrimp with Black Bean Sauce 95
- Sweet and Pungent Shrimp 96
- Shrimp Scampi 97
- Shrimp Amandine 98
- Scampi al Gorgonzola 99
- Shrimp with Amaretto-Cream 100
- Seafood Bake 101
- Shrimp Divan 102
- Shrimp and Stuffed Egg Casserole 103

Shrimp Creole

INGREDIENTS (serves 4)

1/4	Cup	Olive (or vegetable) oil (or bacon drippings)
2	Medium	Onions, sliced
1		Green bell pepper, stem and seeds removed, cut into strips
2	Tbsps.	Flour
1	Can	Tomatoes (16 ounces)
1	Can	Tomato sauce (12 ounces)
1	Tsp.	Oregano
1/2	Tsp.	Salt
1/4	Tsp.	Cayenne pepper
1		Bay leaf
1	Pound	Medium raw shrimp
4	Cups	Hot, fluffy rice

DIRECTIONS

- Heat the oil in a skillet. Add onions and green pepper. Saute for about 3 minutes, stirring frequently, until tender.

- Blend in the flour. Add tomatoes, tomato sauce, oregano, salt, Cayenne and bay leaf. Cover and cook over low heat for about 20 minutes, stirring periodically.

- While the sauce gently simmers, shell and devein the shrimp. Wash under running water and allow to drain.

- Remove the bay leaf and add the shrimp. Mix well and allow to simmer for 3 to 5 minutes, just until the shrimp turn pink.

- Serve over hot, fluffy rice.

The key flavor in this dish is the sherry.

Shrimp Newburg

INGREDIENTS (serves 4)

3		Egg yolks
2	Cups	Cream
3/4	Cup	Butter
2	Tbsps.	Flour
1/4	Cup	Dry sherry
1/8	Tsp.	Nutmeg
1/8	Tsp.	Paprika
1/2	Tsp.	Salt
1 1/2	Pounds	Shrimp, cooked, shelled and deveined, cut into bite-sized pieces
		Buttered bread crumbs

DIRECTIONS

- Beat egg yolks slightly and add to cream. Mix well.

- Melt the butter in a 2 quart saucepan over low heat. Stir in the flour. Add the sherry, a little at a time, while stirring constantly.

- Add the egg-cream mixture to the sherry in the saucepan, a little at a time, while stirring constantly, until a smooth sauce has formed.

- Stir in the nutmeg, paprika and salt. Allow sauce to simmer gently for 5 minutes, stirring periodically.

- Stir in the shrimp and reheat. Spoon into individual ramekins or baking shells. Sprinkle with buttered bread crumbs.

- Broil, about 6" from heat source, for a few minutes, until hot and bubbly. Serve immediately.

Shrimp Rarebit

INGREDIENTS (serves 4)

1	Tbsp.	Butter
1/2	Cup	Milk, ale or beer
1/2	Tsp.	Powdered mustard
1	Pinch	Cayenne pepper
1	Tsp.	Worcestershire sauce
3/4	Pound	Mild white American cheese, coarsely grated
1	Cup	Cooked shrimp, cut into 1/2" pieces
1/4	Cup	Green bell pepper, diced
1	Tbsp.	Onion, diced

DIRECTIONS

- Heat the butter, milk, mustard, cayenne and Worcestershire sauce in the top of a double boiler or chafing dish over just simmering water for 7 to 10 minutes.

- Add the cheese, a little at a time, stirring constantly, until smooth and quite thick.

- Add shrimp, pepper and onion, and cook until thoroughly heated.

- Remove from heat immediately and serve over hot buttered toast points.

Here's just one of the infinite varieties of this wonderful Spanish dish.

Shrimp Paella

INGREDIENTS (serves 4)

1	Tbsp.	Olive oil or salad oil
1/2	Pound	Chorizo (Spanish sausage) or Polish sausage, sliced 1/4" thick
1	Medium	Onion, cut into 8 segments
1	Clove	Garlic, minced
1	Can	Condensed chicken broth (10 3/4 ounces)
1	Can	Tomatoes (8 ounces), chopped
1 1/2	Cups	Long grained rice
1/2	Tsp.	Cinnamon
1/4	Tsp.	Saffron
1/2	Tsp.	Salt
1/4	Tsp.	Black pepper, freshly ground
1/2	Pound	Medium, raw shrimp, shelled and deveined
1	Cup	Frozen peas

DIRECTIONS

- Pour the oil into a medium sized skillet, over medium to high heat. Add the sausage, onion and garlic. Saute until sausage has browned, about 5 minutes.

- Add broth, tomatoes, rice, cinnamon, saffron (crumble it with your fingers as you add it to the skillet), salt and pepper. Heat to boiling, turn down heat, stir once, cover and simmer gently for 15 minutes.

- Quickly add shrimp and peas to top of rice, but do not stir. Recover and simmer for 5 minutes more.

- Transfer to a serving dish, fluffing up the rice and mixing in the shrimp and peas in the process.

For a mild curry flavor, use the amount specified. For a stronger flavor, increase amount according to taste.

Shrimp Curry

INGREDIENTS (serves 4)

1 1/2	Pounds	Uncooked shrimp (or two, 12 ounce packages frozen shrimp)
6	Cups	Boiling water
1	Tbsp.	Salt
1		Bay leaf
2	Slices	Lemon, cut thin
1	Small	Onion, sliced
1/4	Cup	Butter
1	Large	Onion, chopped fine
1		Apple, cored and diced fine
2	Stalks	Celery, chopped fine
1	Cup	Raisins
1	Tbsp.	Curry powder
1	Tsp.	Salt
2	Tbsps.	Flour

DIRECTIONS

- Shell and devein the shrimp. Cook for 4 minutes in simmering water with salt, bay leaf, lemon slices and sliced onion.
- Remove from heat. Drain shrimp and reserve 2 1/2 cups of the shrimp stock.
- Melt butter in a medium saucepan. Add onion and saute just until tender, about 5 minutes.
- Add the apple, celery, raisins, curry powder, salt and flour. Stir to mix ingredients.
- Add reserved shrimp stock and cook over low heat, stirring constantly, until sauce thickens. Continue to cook for an additional 10 minutes to blend flavors.
- Add shrimp to sauce and cook just until shrimp are hot, about 5 minutes.
- Serve with hot cooked rice and condiments such as chutney (buy it bottled), crushed pineapple, chopped salted peanuts, grated coconut, diced cucumber, or chopped hard-cooked eggs.

When serving Shrimp de Jonghe, say "Jonghe" like "wrong". But it sure isn't wrong to serve this famous and delicious dish!

Shrimp de Jonghe

INGREDIENTS (serves 6)

2	Pounds	Shrimp, raw and unshelled
1/4	Cup	Lemon juice (1 lemon)
1	Stalk	Celery, chopped
1	Small	Onion, chopped
2		Bay leaves
1/2	Cup	Butter, softened
1	Cup	Soft bread crumbs
1/4	Cup	Dairy sour cream
1/4	Cup	Parsley flakes
2	Cloves	Garlic, minced
1	Tsp.	Worcestershire sauce
1	Tsp.	Bottled steak sauce
1	Tsp.	Salt
1/4	Tsp.	Black pepper, freshly ground

DIRECTIONS

- Put 6 cups of water in a large saucepan. Add 2 tablespoons of lemon juice, the celery, onion and bay leaves. Bring to a boil, add shrimp and cover. Return to a boil, reduce heat and simmer gently until shrimp turn pink, about 3 minutes. Remove from heat and allow to cool in cooking liquid.

- Cream butter with bread crumbs, sour cream, parsley flakes, garlic, remaining 2 tablespoons of lemon juice, Worcestershire sauce, steak sauce, salt and pepper.

- Drain, shell and devein the cooled shrimp. Arrange shrimp in 6 individual casserole dishes. Cover shrimp with butter mixture.

- Bake, in a preheated 400° oven, until shrimp are heated through, about 15 minutes. Serve hot.

Shrimp-Crab Meat Fondue in Garlicky Bread Cups

INGREDIENTS (serves 6 to 8)

1/2	Pound	Fresh mushrooms
1	Pound	Fresh (or frozen) raw shrimp
1/2	Cup	Butter
1/2	Cup	Scallions, chopped
1	Clove	Garlic, finely diced
5	Tbsps.	Flour
1	Can	Frozen Condensed Cream of Shrimp Soup (10 ounces), thawed
1	Cup	Half-and-half
3/4	Cup	Dry white wine
1/2	Pound	Crab meat
1	Cup	Cheddar cheese, grated
1/8	Tsp.	Cayenne pepper
1/2	Tsp.	Salt
1/4	Tsp.	Black pepper, freshly ground
2	Tbsps.	Fresh parsley, chopped
12		Garlicky bread cups

DIRECTIONS

- Clean the mushrooms, as required, by wiping the tops with a dampened paper towel. Trim off the bottom of each stem and discard. Slice the mushrooms lengthwise.

- Thaw the shrimp if frozen. Shell and devein the shrimp. Wash them in running water and pat dry with paper towels.

- In a large skillet, fry pan or dutch oven, melt the butter. Add the mushrooms, scallions and garlic. Saute for about 5 minutes, until tender.

- Sprinkle the mixture with flour, stir well, and then add the soup, half-and-half and wine. Simmer gently, while stirring, for about 2 minutes.

- Stir in the shrimp, crab meat, all but 1 tablespoon of the Cheddar cheese, the cayenne, salt and pepper. Cover and simmer gently until shrimp are pink, about 3 minutes. Taste and add a bit more salt if required.

- Transfer the mixture to a fondue pot or chafing dish. Garnish with a sprinkling of parsley flakes and the reserved grated Cheddar.

- Spoon shrimp over the bread cups and serve.

Garlicky Bread Cups

INGREDIENTS (makes 12 cups)

12	Slices	Fresh white bread
4	Ounces	Butter (1 stick)
1	Tsp.	Garlic powder
1/4	Tsp.	Salt

DIRECTIONS

- Trim the crusts from bread.

- Melt the butter in a small saucepan. Season with garlic and salt. With a pastry brush, spread the garlic butter over both sides of the bread.

- Press each slice into a cup in a muffin tin, so that the corners turn up.

- Bake, in a preheated 300° oven, for 35 to 40 minutes, until bread cups are crispy.

Stir Fried Shrimp and Pea Pods

INGREDIENTS (serves 4)

1	Pound	Medium, raw shrimp
1	Tbsp.	Cornstarch
2	Tbsps.	Soy sauce
2	Tbsps.	Dry sherry
2	Tbsps.	Fresh ginger
4	Cloves	Garlic, minced
1/2	Cup	Water
2	Tbsps.	Salad oil
1/2	Pound	Mushrooms, sliced
1/2	Pound	Edible pea pods (sugar, snap or Oriental), strings pulled off
4		Green onions (with tops), cut into thin diagonal slices

DIRECTIONS

- Peel the shrimp, but leave last section of tail intact. Devein the shrimp, rinse them in cold running water and pat dry with paper towels.

- Combine the cornstarch, soy sauce, sherry, ginger, garlic and water.

- In a wok or large frying pan, over medium high heat, combine the oil and mushrooms. Stir-fry until mushrooms begin to get limp, about 2 minutes.

- Add the shrimp and the cornstarch mixture. Stir constantly until shrimp are pink and liquid is thickened, about 4 minutes.

- Add pea pods and stir until hot.

- Transfer to a serving dish, sprinkle with green onion and serve at once with hot, fluffy rice.

Shrimp with Black Bean Sauce

INGREDIENTS (serves 4)

1	Pound	Medium, fresh shrimp
1		Egg white (or 1 tablespoon cornstarch)
2	Cups	Vegetable oil
1	Tbsp.	Fermented black beans
3	Cloves	Garlic, minced
1	Tsp.	Fresh ginger, minced
1	Small	Dried Chinese red pepper, (optional) minced
1/8	Tsp.	Salt
1		Green bell pepper, stem and seeds removed, cut into 1" squares
2	Tbsps.	Chicken broth
2	Tbsps.	Soy sauce
2	Tbsps.	White wine
1	Tsp.	Cornstarch, mixed with 1/4 cup water
1	Tbsp.	Scallions, minced

DIRECTIONS

- Shell and devein the shrimp. Wash them and thoroughly dry with paper towels. Place them in a bowl and add the egg white (or cornstarch) and 1/2 teaspoon vegetable oil. Toss to coat and allow to marinate for 5 minutes.

- Wash the black beans and mash slightly with your fingers.

- Heat a wok over highest heat for 2 minutes. When hot, add the remaining vegetable oil. As soon as oil is smoking hot, fry the shrimp for a few seconds, only until they turn white. Remove shrimp quickly from wok and let oil drain off.

- Clean the wok, reheat it and add 3 tablespoons of the vegetable oil. When oil is smoking hot, add the black beans, garlic, ginger, red pepper and salt, mashing them all together.

SHRIMP WITH BLACK BEAN SAUCE (continued)

- Add the green bell pepper, chicken broth, and soy sauce. Stir fry for 30 seconds. Return shrimp to wok and add wine. Stir for 10 seconds. Add cornstarch mixture and stir until the sauce thickens and clears, about 10 seconds.

- Transfer to a serving dish, sprinkle with scallions and serve hot.

Sweet and Pungent Shrimp

INGREDIENTS (serves 4)

1	Pound	Shrimp, fresh or frozen
1	Can	Pineapple chunks (8 ounces)
1/2	Cup	Brown sugar
1/2	Cup	Vinegar
2	Tbsps.	Soy sauce
2	Tbsps.	Cornstarch
1		Green bell pepper, stem and seeds removed, cut into 1" pieces
1		Tomato, cut into wedges, wedges cut in half

DIRECTIONS

- Cook the shrimp. Shell, devein and rinse under cool, running water. Pat dry with paper towels.

- Drain the syrup from pineapple into a 2 quart saucepan. Reserve the pineapple chunks. Add the sugar, vinegar, soy sauce and 1 cup of water to the pineapple syrup. Bring to a boil.

- Combine cornstarch and 1/4 cup of water. Add to pineapple juice mixture. Cook, stirring constantly, until thickened.

- Add the green pepper, tomato and reserved pineapple. Cook for 2 minutes. Add shrimp and cook to heat the shrimp through. Serve immediately.

The Italian word for shrimp is scampi, so the title of this famous dish is really "Shrimp Shrimp". (Or, in Italian, "Scampi Scampi".) However, it isn't only Italians who know that it's delizioso!

Shrimp Scampi (Garlic-broiled Shrimp)

INGREDIENTS (serves 4)

1 1/2	Pounds	Large, raw shrimp
1/2	Cup	Butter, melted
1/2	Cup	Olive oil
2	Tsps.	Lemon juice
2		Green onions, chopped fine
2	Cloves	Garlic, finely diced
2	Tbsps.	Parsley flakes
1/2	Tsp.	Salt
1/4	Tsp.	Black pepper, freshly ground
		Lemon wedges

DIRECTIONS

- Shell and devein the shrimp. Wash under running water and pat dry with paper towels.

- In the bottom of a broiling pan, combine the butter, olive oil, lemon juice, green onions, garlic, parsley flakes, salt and pepper.

- Add the shrimp, turning them in the mixture to coat all sides. Arrange shrimp in a single layer.

- Broil, about 5 inches from heat, turning once and basting often with marinade, until shrimp are opaque and curled, about 5 to 8 minutes.

- To serve, spoon shrimp and pan juices onto a warm platter. Garnish with lemon wedges.

NOTE

- If desired, leave the tip of the tail attached when shelling the shrimp to use as a handle.

Shrimp Amandine

INGREDIENTS (serves 4)

1/2	Cup	Butter
1	Cup	Blanched, slivered almonds
1	Pound	Raw shrimp, shelled and deveined
1/2	Tsp.	Salt
1/8	Tsp.	Black pepper, freshly ground
2	Tbsps.	Parsley flakes
		Toast points

DIRECTIONS

- Melt butter in a medium skillet. Add almonds and saute until light brown. Remove almonds with a slotted spoon and reserve.

- Add shrimp and saute until cooked, about 3 or 4 minutes.

- Add salt, pepper, parsley and toasted almonds. Stir together thoroughly and serve on toast points.

Scampi al Gorgonzola

INGREDIENTS (serves 4)

2	Pounds	Medium raw shrimp in shells (preferably with heads on)
1 1/2	Tbsps.	Cooking oil
1	Medium	Onion, chopped
1/2	Tsp.	Salt
1/4	Tsp.	Black pepper, freshly ground
1/2	Cup	Dry white wine
		Flour for dredging
4	Tbsps.	Butter
2	Ounces	Gorgonzola cheese, crumbled
3	Tbsps.	Fresh bread crumbs

DIRECTIONS

- Remove heads and shells from shrimp. Set heads and shells aside. Devein the shrimp. Wash shrimp and pat dry with paper towels.

- In a medium skillet, heat the oil. Add the onion and saute until golden. Add the reserved heads and shells. Season with the salt and pepper, and add the wine. Simmer for about 5 minutes. Allow to cool, then press the mixture into the bottom of a fine sieve, extracting all of the shrimp flavored liquid. Reserve.

- Dredge shrimp lightly in flour.

- Heat 3 tablespoons of the butter in a small skillet. Saute the shrimp, a few at a time, until golden. Arrange the shrimp in a shallow baking dish. Pour any butter remaining into the reserved shrimp flavored liquid.

- Heat the reserved shrimp liquid in a small saucepan. Add the cheese and stir constantly until sauce is smooth. Pour the sauce over the shrimp and sprinkle with bread crumbs. Dot with the remaining butter.

- Broil, about 4 inches from heat source, for 1 to 2 minutes, until browned on top.

Shrimp with Amaretto-Cream

INGREDIENTS (serves 2)

3/4	Pound	Large shrimp, raw
2	Tsps.	Butter
1	Tbsp.	Shallots (or onion, finely diced
2	Tbsps.	Sweet red peppers, diced
2	Tsps.	Madras curry powder
2	Tbsps.	Dry white wine
4	Tsps.	Amaretto (almond flavored liqueur)
1/2	Pint	Heavy cream
2	Tsps.	Parsley flakes
1/8	Tsp.	Salt
1/8	Tsp.	Black pepper, freshly ground
1	Ounce	Split almonds, toasted until golden brown

DIRECTIONS

- Shell and devein the shrimp. Rinse them and pat dry with paper towels.

- Melt the butter in a medium frying pan. Add the shallots and saute for several minutes, until they become transparent but not brown.

- Add the shrimp and turn them about in the pan for a minute or so.

- Pour in the wine and add the peppers. Heat until liquid is reduced by half.

- Add the curry powder and Amaretto. Cook for 30 seconds. Stir in the cream and half the parsley. Cook for 2 minutes.

- Season with the salt and pepper. If the sauce seems to be too thick, thin it with a bit more wine.

- Transfer to a warm serving dish, and garnish with the toasted almonds and the remaining parsley. Serve with hot, fluffy rice.

Seafood Bake

INGREDIENTS (serves 8 to 10)

3/4	Cup	Butter
1	Pound	Fresh mushrooms, cleaned and sliced
6	Tbsps.	Flour
1	Tsp.	Salt
1/2	Tsp.	Black pepper, freshly ground
3	Cups	Half and half
1/2	Cup	Sharp Cheddar cheese (2 ounces), shredded
1/4	Tsp.	Worcestershire sauce
2	Pounds	Shrimp, cooked, shelled and deveined
1 to 2	Cups	Lump crab meat, cartilage removed
1/4	Cup	Dry sherry
1	Cup	Bread crumbs
1/4	Cup	Butter, melted

DIRECTIONS

- Melt the butter in a large skillet. Add mushrooms and saute until tender, 3 to 4 minutes.

- Add the flour, salt and pepper. Stir well and cook until mixture begins to bubble.

- Reduce heat to low and gradually add the half and half, a little at a time, until sauce has thickened.

- Add the cheese and Worcestershire sauce, and stir until cheese melts. Blend in the shrimp, crab and sherry.

- Pour mixture into a 9x12" casserole dish. Combine bread crumbs and butter. Sprinkle over the mixture.

- Bake, in a preheated 350° oven, for 40 to 45 minutes, or until hot and bubbly.

If you enjoy Chicken Divan, you'll want to try this dish.

Shrimp Divan

INGREDIENTS (serves 4 to 6)

2	Packages	Frozen broccoli (10 ounces each) cooked as package directs
1	Pound	Shrimp, cooked, shelled and deveined
1/2	Tsp.	Salt
1/4	Tsp.	Black pepper, fresh ground
1	Can	Condensed cream of celery soup (10 1/2 ounces)
1	Cup	Mayonnaise
1	Tsp.	Lemon juice
1/2	Cup	Cheddar cheese, shredded
1/2	Cup	Seasoned bread crumbs
1/4	Cup	Butter, melted

DIRECTIONS

- Grease a shallow casserole dish. Place chopped broccoli in the bottom, and arrange shrimp on top. Sprinkle with salt and pepper.

- Mix the soup with the mayonnaise, lemon juice and cheese. Pour this mixture over the shrimp.

- Mix bread crumbs with melted butter and sprinkle on the top.

- Bake, in a preheated 350° oven, for 30 minutes.

Here's a dish that will surprise your diners.

Shrimp and Stuffed Egg Casserole

INGREDIENTS (serves 4)

4		Hard-cooked eggs
1	Tbsp.	Onion, finely diced
1	Tsp.	Dry mustard
1/4	Tsp.	Salt
1/8	Tsp.	Black pepper, freshly ground
1	Dash	Paprika
		Mayonnaise
1	Pound	Shrimp, cooked, shelled and deveined
3	Tbsps.	Butter
2	Tbsps.	Flour
1 1/2	Cups	Milk
1/8	Cup	Dried bread crumbs
1	Tbsp.	Butter, melted

DIRECTIONS

- Halve the eggs lengthwise. Remove yolks and pass through a sieve. Add onion, mustard, salt, pepper, paprika and just enough mayonnaise to blend (2 or 3 tablespoons). Fill egg whites with egg yolk mixture. Arrange in the bottom of a buttered 1 1/2 quart casserole.

- Arrange shrimp on top of the stuffed eggs.

- Melt the butter over medium heat in a small saucepan. Stir in the flour. Add the milk, a little at a time, while stirring continually, until a smooth sauce has formed. Pour this sauce over the shrimp and stuffed eggs. Do not stir.

- Combine bread crumbs and melted butter. Sprinkle over the sauce.

- Bake, in a preheated 375° oven, for 20 minutes, or until casserole is bubbling and top is brown.

Sauces to Dip Your Shrimp

- Seafood Dip 106
- Shrimp Dip 106
- Louis Dressing 107
- Garlic Mayonnaise 107
- Mustard Mayonnaise 108
- Tartar Sauce 108
- Caper Sauce 109
- French Dressing 109
- Curry Dip 110
- Mustard Cocktail Sauce 110
- Marmalade and Mustard Sauce 111
- Chinese Hot Mustard 111
- Fruit Sauce 112
- Hot Apricot Sauce 112

Seafood Dip

INGREDIENTS (makes 3 cups)

1 1/2	Cups	Mayonnaise or salad dressing
1	Cup	Catsup
1/2	Cup	Grated Parmesan cheese
1	Tbsp.	Parsley flakes
1	Tsp.	Seasoned salt
		Boiled shrimp, crabs, or crawfish

DIRECTIONS

- In a bowl combine the mayonnaise, catsup, cheese, parsley flakes and salt. Cover and chill.

- Serve with boiled shrimp, crabs, or crawfish.

Shrimp Dip

INGREDIENTS (makes about 1 cup)

1	Cup	Mayonnaise
3/4	Tsp.	Curry powder
1/4	Tsp.	Chili powder
1	Clove	Garlic, minced
1/4	Cup	Chili sauce

DIRECTIONS

- In a small bowl, mix all ingredients until well combined.

- Refrigerate until ready to serve. Serve as a dip for cold cooked shrimp.

Louis Dressing

INGREDIENTS (makes about 3 cups)

2	Cups	Mayonnaise
2/3	Cup	Chili sauce
3	Tbsps.	Cider vinegar
3	Tbsps.	Parsley flakes
4	Tsps.	Horseradish
1	Tsp.	Worcestershire sauce

DIRECTIONS

- Combine all ingredients. Pour into plastic container. Cover and refrigerate until well chilled.

Ah . . . just smell that fresh garlic!

Garlic Mayonnaise

INGREDIENTS (makes 1/2 cup)

1/2	Cup	Mayonnaise
1	Large	Clove garlic, peeled

DIRECTIONS

- Place mayonnaise in small bowl. Put garlic into press and squeeze over mayonnaise.

- Mix well and serve within an hour or two.

Mustard Mayonnaise

INGREDIENTS (makes 3/4 cup)

1/2	Cup	Mayonnaise
1	Tsp.	Dijon-style mustard
3	Tbsps.	Heavy cream
1/4	Tsp.	Lemon juice
1/4	Tsp.	Salt
1/8	Tsp.	Black pepper, freshly ground

DIRECTIONS

- Combine all ingredients. Blend well and serve.

Tartar Sauce

INGREDIENTS (makes 1 1/4 cups)

1	Cup	Mayonnaise
2	Tbsps.	Onion, chopped
1	Tbsp.	Dill pickle, chopped (or pickle relish, drained)
1	Tbsp.	Parsley flakes
1	Tbsp.	Chopped chives
1	Tbsp.	Capers, chopped
1	Tsp.	Prepared mustard
1/4	Tsp.	Salt
1/8	tsp.	Black pepper, freshly ground

DIRECTIONS

- Combine all ingredients in a small mixing bowl. Cover and chill until ready to use.

Caper Sauce

INGREDIENTS (makes about 1 1/4 cups)

1/2	Cup	Mayonnaise
1/2	Cup	Commercial sour cream
2	Tbsps.	Capers, chopped
2	Tbsps.	Prepared mustard
4	Drops	Tabasco sauce

DIRECTIONS

- Combine all ingredients and mix thoroughly. Serve with deep fried shrimp.

French Dressing

INGREDIENTS (makes about 1 cup)

3/4	Cup	Salad oil
1/4	Cup	Lemon juice or cider vinegar
1	Tbsp.	Sugar
3/4	Tsp.	Salt
1/4	Tsp.	Paprika
1/4	Tsp.	Dry mustard
1/4	Tsp.	Black pepper, freshly ground

DIRECTIONS

- Combine all ingredients in a screw top pint jar. Cover tightly and shake vigorously.

- Store covered in refrigerator. Shake well before using.

Curry Dip

INGREDIENTS (makes 1 cup)

1	Cup	Dairy sour cream
3/4	Tsp.	Curry powder
1/4	Tsp.	Salt

DIRECTIONS

- Combine all ingredients and mix well. Refrigerate until time to serve.

Mustard Cocktail Sauce

INGREDIENTS (makes about 3/4 cup)

2	Tbsps.	Cider vinegar
6	Tbsps.	Olive oil
3	Tbsps.	Prepared Dijon-style mustard
1	Clove	Garlic, minced
3	Fillets	Anchovy, minced
1/2	Tsp.	Salt
1	Tbsp.	Chopped chives (or scallion tops)
1	Tbsp.	Parsley flakes
1		Egg, hard cooked and mashed

DIRECTIONS

- Combine all ingredients in a small jar which has a tight fitting cover. Shake well and place in freezer for 30 minutes. Remove and again shake well, until all ingredients are thoroughly blended.

- Serve with cooked, shelled, deveined and chilled shrimp.

Marmalade and Mustard Sauce

INGREDIENTS (makes about 1/2 cup)

1/2	Cup	Orange marmalade
1	Tsp.	Chinese Hot Mustard
1	Tsp.	Grand Marnier Liquor

DIRECTIONS

- Combine all ingredients, stir well and serve.

Chinese Hot Mustard

INGREDIENTS (makes about 1/4 cup)

4	Tbsps.	Dry mustard
1/2	Tsp.	Salt
2	Tbsps.	Cider vinegar (or more)
2	Drops	Tabasco sauce

DIRECTIONS

- Place mustard in a small sauce dish. Add salt.

- Add vinegar, a little at a time, while stirring, until a smooth thin sauce has been made. Add a drop or two of Tabasco sauce.

- Allow to stand for 20 minutes to develop flavor.

NOTE

- This sauce is hot and can be made hotter with more Tabasco sauce.

- Place any sauce remaining after the meal into a small jar and refrigerate. Add more vinegar to re-thin sauce before next using.

Fruit Sauce

INGREDIENTS (makes about 1 cup)

3/4	Cup	Orange marmalade
2	Tbsps.	Lemon juice
2	Tbsps.	Orange juice
2	Tsps.	Grated horseradish
1/2	Tsp.	Ground ginger

DIRECTIONS

- Combine all ingredients in a blender and mix at low speed for 1 minute. Serve with deep fried shrimp.

Hot Apricot Sauce

INGREDIENTS (makes about 2 cups)

1/2	Cup	Pineapple juice
1/4	Cup	Dry mustard
2	Tbsps.	Soy sauce
1	Cup	Apricot preserves
1		Lemon

DIRECTIONS

- In the top of a double boiler, over boiling water, combine the pineapple juice, dry mustard, soy sauce, apricot preserves, and the juice and grated peel of the lemon. Stir ingredients together and heat until hot.

- Serve either hot or cold.

Detailed Contents

INTRODUCTION VI
   What Shrimp Are! VI
   What Types are Available? . . VII
   Where are They Caught
     In the U.S.? VII
   When Can They be
     Purchased? VII
   In What Forms are They
     Sold? VII
   What Sizes are Sold? VIII
   Grading of Shrimp! VIII
   What Size Should I
     Purchase? IX
   How Much Should I Buy? . . IX
   How Do I Check for
     Freshness? X
   How Long Will They Last? . . X
   When to Remove the Shell! . . XI
   To Remove the Shell! XI
   To Devein Shrimp! XI
   To Butterfly Shrimp! XII
   What are the Qualities of
     Well Cooked Shrimp? XII
   Salt, Pepper and Butter. . . XII

BASICS OF COOKING
SHRIMP 1
   Cooking Shrimp Before
     Removing Shells 3
   Cooking Shrimp After
     Removing Shells 4
   Hot & Spicy Steamed Shrimp. . . 5
   Shrimp Boil 7
   Garithes (Shrimp) in Shells. . . 8
   Shrimp Cooked in Court
     Bouillion 9
   Shrimp Shell Broth 10

APPETIZERS . . SERVED HOT 11
   Shrimp & Cheese Canapes . . 12
   Shrimp Stuffed with Crab
     Meat 13

Shrimp Rumaki 14
Shrimp Toast 15
APPETIZERS .. SERVED COLD 17
   Shrimp and Vegetable
     Appetizer 18
   Stuffed Shrimp Canape 19
   Roquefort Stuffed Shrimp . . 20
   Shrimp Stuffed Eggs 21
   Shrimp Stuffed Celery 22
   Shrimp Pate 22
   Shrimp Butter 23
PICKLED & MARINATED. . . . 25
   Pickled Shrimp 26
   Marinated Shrimp 27
   Italian Style Marinated
     Shrimp 28
   Deviled Shrimp 29
   Cold Spiced Szechwan
     Shrimp 30
THE FIRST COURSE 31
   Shrimp Cocktail 32
     Seafood Cocktail Sauce . . . 33
   Shrimp Remoulade 34
   Mushroom and Shrimp
     Cocktail 35
   Garlic Shrimp 36
   Baked Garlicky Breaded
     Shrimp 37
   King Stuffed Shrimp 38
BISQUES, GUMBO,
JAMBALAYA 39
   Shrimp Bisque 40
   Shrimp Bisque, Traditional . . 41
   Shrimp Gumbo 42
   Shrimp Jambalaya 44
SALADS 47
   Shrimp Salad 48
   Stuffed Tomato Salad 49

Shrimp in Avocado Halves . . 50
Party Shrimp Salad 51
Shrimp & Macaroni Salad . . . 52
Shrimp & Pineapple Salad . . . 53
Shrimp Mousse 54
SANDWICHES 55
Shrimp Salad 56
Shrimp-Avocado Club 57
Ham and Baby Shrimp 58
Broiled Shrimp 59
Shrimp, Bacon and Cheese . . . 60
Shrimpburgers 61
COOKED ON THE GRILL 63
Barbecued Shrimp 64
Shrimp en Brochette 65
Chinese Skewered Shrimp . . . 66
Shrimp Kebabs 67
DEEP FAT FRIED
FAVORITES 69
French Fried Shrimp 70
Deep Fried Butterfly Shrimp 71
Shrimp in Beer Batter 72
Fried Shrimp in Cornmeal . . 73
Shrimp Tempura 74
Szechwan Spicy Shrimp. 76
Hawaiian Shrimp Luau 78
Crab Meat Stuffed Shrimp. . . 79
Shrimp Croquettes 80
Philippine Egg Rolls 82
  Egg Roll Wrappers 84
SHRIMPLY DELICIOUS MAIN
DISHES 85
Shrimp Creole 86
Shrimp Newburg 87
Shrimp Rarebit 88
Shrimp Paella 89
Shrimp Curry 90
Shrimp de Jonghe 91
Shrimp-Crab Meat Fondue
 in Garlicky Bread Cups . . . 92
   Garlicky Bread Cups 93

Stir Fried Shrimp & Pea Pods 94
Shrimp with Black Bean
  Sauce 95
Sweet and Pungent Shrimp . . 96
Shrimp Scampi 97
Shrimp Amandine 98
Scampi al Gorgonzola 99
Shrimp with Amaretto
  Cream 100
Seafood Bake 101
Shrimp Divan 102
Shrimp & Stuffed Egg
  Casserole 103
SAUCES TO DIP YOUR
SHRIMP 105
Seafood Dip 106
Shrimp Dip 106
Louis Dressing 107
Garlic Mayonnaise 107
Mustard Mayonnaise 108
Tartar Sauce 108
Caper Sauce 109
French Dressing 109
Curry Dip 110
Mustard Cocktail Sauce. . . . 110
Marmalade & Mustard Sauce 111
Chinese Hot Mustard 111
Fruit Sauce 112
Hot Apricot Sauce 112